P9-BTN-094

Girls
AND
YOUNG
WOMEN
Leading the Way

20
TRUE STORIES ABOUT
LEADERSHIP

FRANCES A. KARNES, PH.D. AND
SUZANNE M. BEAN, PH.D.

EDITED BY ROSEMARY WALLNER

Free Spirit
PUBLISHING

FRANKLIN PIERCE
COLLEGE LIBRARY
RINDGE, N.H. 03461

Copyright © 1993 by Frances A. Karnes and Suzanne M. Bean
All rights reserved. Unless otherwise noted, no part of this book may be
reproduced in any form, except for brief reviews, without written permission
of the publisher.

Library of Congress Cataloging-in-Publication Data
Karnes, Frances A.
    Girls and young women leading the way : 20 true stories about
leadership / Frances A. Karnes and Suzanne M. Bean.
        p.   cm.
    Includes bibliographical references and index.
    Summary: Recounts the experiences of twenty girls and young
women who have led the way in such community action as feeding the
hungry, recycling, saving the bluebirds, and promoting literacy.
    ISBN 0-915793-52-0
    1. Youth volunteers in community development—United States—
Case studies—Juvenile literature. 2. Student volunteers in social
service—United States—Case studies—Juvenile literature. 3. Women in
community development—United States—Case studies—Juvenile literature. 4. Leadership—Case studies—Juvenile literature. [1. Volunteer
workers in social service. 2. Voluntarism. 3. Women in community
development. 4. Leadership.] I. Bean, Suzanne M., 1957–   . II. Title.
    HN90.V64K37 1993
    361.3'7'0835—dc20   93-25874
                                                                      CIP
                                                                      AC

Cover and book design by MacLean & Tuminelly
Editorial direction by Pamela Espeland
Index prepared by Eileen Quam and Theresa Wolner
10 9 8 7 6 5 4 3 2
Printed in the United States of America

Free Spirit Publishing Inc.
400 First Avenue North, Suite 616
Minneapolis, MN 55401
(612) 338-2068

CORR
HN
90
. V64
C37
1993

The five messages about leadership from Women in Power—The Secrets of
Leadership by Dorothy Cantor and Toni Bernay (Houghton Mifflin Company,
1992) on pages 132–134 are included with permission of the copyright
holder.
All organization names and addresses included in this book are current and
accurate as of March 1993.

Dedication

This book is dedicated to our mothers, Carlene H. Nessler and Maxine P. Meriweather, who taught us to believe in ourselves and who have had a significant, positive influence on the development of our own leadership potential.

Additionally, this book is dedicated to all the young female leaders who deeply enrich our society and who give us reason to celebrate leadership.

Acknowledgments

The vision, goal setting, and accomplishments of girls and young women around the country have made this book a reality. All of the young women highlighted in this book have empowered themselves to be leaders. They did not wait to be appointed or elected to a position of leadership. Instead, they saw an opportunity to initiate or change something in their school or community, and they took action. We deeply appreciate their leadership abilities and their willingness to share their stories with others. To the many students across the United States who sent stories for consideration, we thank you and congratulate you on your accomplishments.

We are grateful to the many organizations, associations, and individuals who responded to our search for young leaders. Without the help of hundreds of adults, the girls and young women who shared their experiences would not have been identified. We are indebted to the administrators, faculty, and staff of the University of Southern Mississippi and the Mississippi University for Women who continue to assist and support our work in the area of leadership development of youth. We are indebted to the superintendent and the staff of the Meridian Public Schools and to the Jeff Anderson Regional Medical Center staff. Both provided convenient and comfortable space for the work sessions that took place midway between our home offices.

To the nation's outstanding female leaders whose statements are quoted in the Leadership Handbook section, we owe a special thanks. These distinguished leaders are excellent role models whose accomplishments and expressions will inspire young prospective female leaders for years to come.

To our publisher, Judy Galbraith, we express with enthusiasm our respect and admiration, not only for her many inspiring leadership qualities, but also for her patience with two busy authors. Leanne Halford and Penelope-Mariah Sheehan provided the selected readings and technical assistance. We extend our special appreciation to them. We give a huge thank you to the secretaries, Linda Meylan, Stacey Burnett, and Liz Trego, who gave their special assistance and expertise to the manuscript. Very deepest appreciation is expressed to Caroline Barnes, administrative assistant at The Center for Gifted Studies, who so ably oversees many details.

To E. P., who continues to be a special friend, our deepest gratitude.

To our husbands, Doctors M. Ray Karnes and Mark H. Bean, leaders in their respective fields who are fully appreciative of the joys and tribulations of being husbands of women with strong professional commitments, we express our heartfelt thanks for their continuing love, support, devotion, and patience. For the inspiration they provide and the love and devotion they demonstrate in so many ways, we also thank Christopher and John Karnes and Cameron Meriweather Bean.

Contents

PART THREE: A LEADERSHIP HANDBOOK — **127**

INDEX — **154**

ABOUT THE AUTHORS — **160**

Introduction

MORE THAN WORDS—
LEADERSHIP IN ACTION

*H*AVE YOU EVER DISCOVERED A PROBLEM— in your school or community—that you thought you could solve? Have you ever wanted to start a new school club or gather friends together to share an interest? Have you ever felt that your school or community needed some new way of doing something? What made you act on your ideas? What made you hesitate?

The girls and young women who share their stories in this book had uncertainties and faced obstacles—just as you have in your life. They saw something that needed doing and made sure that something got done. They talked to people and created a plan; they set goals and put their ideas into action. They looked around their schools and communities and identified many problems common in our country and around the world: homelessness, disregard for the environment, poor race relations, inadequate educational opportunities for children and adults, lack of support for the fine and performing arts, and the absence of community improvement programs. The girls and young women in this book faced all sorts of difficulties but stayed with their plans to motivate their peers as well as adults. They focused attention on community and school issues. They gathered resources and found solutions.

Many of these young leaders wrote letters and petitions, gave speeches, and worked with the media. Some projects continued over a long period of time while others took a much shorter time. In some stories, the person who initiated a project trained others to take over her leadership role. Some have received awards for their achievements, but, for them, the act of leading and achieving goals was most important.

At the beginning of each chapter in Part One and Part Two, we wrote short sections introducing you to the girls and young women who share their experiences. As you'll see, they represent a cross-section of our nation. They range in age from eight to twenty-one and are from modest to affluent homes. Some have brothers and sisters, while a few are the only children in their families. Some live with two parents, others with a single parent or grandparent—in other words, they are probably a lot like you and people you know.

HOW TO USE THIS BOOK

If you want to make this book more of your own, we encourage you to record your important ideas and experiences in a Leadership Notebook. Use a tablet of paper, spiral notebook, blank-page book, loose pages in a folder, or even a computer disk. In your notebook, record *your* thoughts about leadership.

In this book, you'll find twenty stories of leaders at work. The first ten stories were written by girls and young women who made a change in their communities. The second ten were written by young leaders who made a change at their school.

Following each story is a "What You Can Do" section. The activities and questions will give you ideas about leadership opportunities in your own community and school. Ask yourself if any of the suggestions seem like something you could do.

• • •

Create a section in your Leadership Notebook titled "My Leadership Plan." Write down activities from the "What You Can Do" sections that you'd like to do. Make a list of other activities you think of as you read the "What You Can Do" sections.

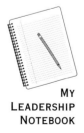

MY LEADERSHIP NOTEBOOK

Once you come up with a plan, you can include your goals, objectives, and a timeline in your notebook. As you work through your plan, you can use your Leadership Notebook to record your accomplishments.

• • •

The "Find Out More, Get Involved" section at the end of each chapter includes names and addresses of national clubs and organizations. Many of these groups have brochures, fliers, and other printed materials that might be helpful as you plan your own leadership project. They can tell you how to start a local chapter of their organization or how to recruit members.

Write letters to any that interest you and keep copies in your notebook. Use your telephone directory or call the mayor's office to find out about local chapters of any groups in which you're interested. Perhaps the telephone book for your state capital, usually available in your local library, will have numbers for state groups. Check your own telephone directory for local organizations.

• • •

Begin a section of your notebook titled "Resources for My Leadership Plan." Identify resources you may need for your leadership plan. Include names, addresses, phone numbers, and other pertinent information.

MY LEADERSHIP NOTEBOOK

• • •

ABOUT THE LEADERSHIP HANDBOOK

Part Three of this book is devoted to you. Reading about the leaders in the first sections will start you thinking about leadership. Reading the Leadership Handbook will inspire you to act on those thoughts.

The Leadership Handbook defines leadership and shares some behind-the-scenes information about how leadership has changed throughout history. The "Women as Leaders: Looking toward the

Future" section predicts some of the trends for women leaders of today. In "Leadership Messages Especially for You," we included some positive messages for all leaders.

We found some interesting quotations on leadership and included them in the chapter titled "What Today's Women Leaders Say About Leadership." (We took some of these from books about famous leaders; others came directly from prominent women of today.) We hope they will inspire you as you develop your own leadership potential.

• • •

My Leadership Notebook

Start a section in your Leadership Notebook titled "My Quotes on Leadership." Record your own ideas about what you think inspires leaders. How can you become inspired? Copy into your notebook any quotes about leadership you find in books, magazines, or newspapers.

• • •

We want you to continue reading and learning about leadership so we included a selected reading list in the chapter "Read More about It: A Leadership Bibliography." This section offers some of the best books about women leaders. By reading about famous leaders, past and present, you'll find out how they faced problems and found solutions. (In the future, perhaps a book about you will be on a reading list!)

To help you find the books that are right for you, we divided the chapter into sections based on reading levels. Think of these reading levels as guidelines only. Don't let them stop you from reading a book that interests you, even if it's "too old" or "too young."

• • •

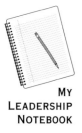

My Leadership Notebook

In a section titled "My Ideas from Read More about It," write down your own ideas for leadership. Read some of the books in the "Read More about It" section and record your thoughts.

• • •

We want you to realize your own potential for leadership. You can read about what others have done and listen to suggestions about what you *should* do. What you *will* do is up to you.

Frances Karnes
Suzanne Bean
Fall 1993

LEADERSHIP IN ACTION:

IN THE COMMUNITY

A community is made up of people—young and old. Anyone in a community who wants to make improvements should be allowed to propose a plan—and that means you, too. Many young people expect leadership experiences in the community to be difficult. They're afraid adults won't take their ideas seriously. But as you'll see in the stories that follow, age has no limit on good ideas and positive action. In each story, a girl or young woman brought attention to a cause and united her peers and adults. These young people found an issue or condition that needed to be changed, improved, or addressed. They knew something had to be done and persisted until they met their goals.

Isis Johnson

LEADERSHIP BEGINS
AT AN EARLY AGE

ISIS JOHNSON *is eight years old and a third-grader at Robert Mills Lusher Magnet School in New Orleans, Louisiana. On weekends and during the summer, she lives with her grandmother, Claudette Jones. Isis likes to jump rope, roller blade, and play with her friends. She also enjoys ballet classes. She hopes to be a dancer and a doctor when she grows up.*

In May 1992, President George Bush named Isis the nation's 779th Point of Light for her work in feeding hungry people in New Orleans. (Bush had established the program to honor people who do outstanding volunteer service in their communities.) In January 1993, Isis was further honored at the White House when she attended a special dinner for all those who had received the Points of Light Award. In addition to winning presidential recognition, Isis was inducted into the Mickey Mouse Hall of Fame. She was the first child in the state of Louisiana to be admitted into that prestigious organization.

In late 1992, the Disney Company filmed a special program about Isis that aired on television in the spring of 1993. Isis has also received numerous awards and commendations at the city, state, and national levels from a long list of noteworthy officials, including a United States Congressman, the Governor of Louisiana, the Louisiana Legislature, the New Orleans City Council, and the Mayor of New Orleans.

I WAS FOUR YEARS OLD WHEN I FIRST FELT the need to help poor people. It began when my grandmother and I were watching television while eating our dinner. A program came on dealing with the starving children in Ethiopia. I felt extremely sorry for those children and asked my grandmother if we could send the rest of the chicken we had in my grandmother's kitchen to those boys and girls. My grandmother explained that it would not be possible, so I asked if there were also children in New Orleans who were hungry. When my grandmother said yes, I said that we should go all over and get people to give us food so we could give it to hungry children, because God did not mean for anyone to be hungry.

I was five when I began going door-to-door collecting food. My grandmother and I made a sign asking for food donations for the poor and hungry. We put the sign in the window of her car, and she drove me around our neighborhood and surrounding areas so I could talk to people about my interest in getting food for the poor. Many people said that they were interested in helping.

They started bringing food to our home so it could be given to those who needed it. Then I thought about how to give the food to people. I talked to my minister. He told people about what I was doing and how I wanted to help. My grandmother told the Salvation Army about what I was doing and they said that they would help to tell needy people. My grandmother and I decided that the food would be given to people at our house on a certain day in December, just before Christmas.

Isis Johnson with some of the food she has collected

One thousand canned items and other foods that didn't spoil were given to many families who were in need. They told me thank you and said how much my idea was going to help them. Several people asked me if I was going to do it again. Of course, I told them that I would continue to get food for the poor.

Many people heard about my work and got interested. There were stories about it on television, radio, and in the newspaper. Lots of people called and wanted to help. A few gave money to buy food, and other people continued to bring food to my house.

The next year, when I was six years old, I helped collect 1,300 items that were given to the poor. I gave the collected food to the Salvation Army. The following year, the number of items given was very big—4,000. I hope that I can do more every year.

When I first began collecting food for the poor, the New Orleans newspaper, *The Times-Picayune*, wrote a story about me. The story was printed in other newspapers across the country. Many people called from all over to talk to me about my projects. Since then, there have been several other stories about me on radio and TV and in the newspaper. I guess that people were surprised at what a little girl could do.

Over the years, there have been other stories besides the one about the children in Ethiopia that have made me sad. I have tried to think of other ways to help people. One day I heard of a child who was shot on the street by someone driving by in a car. How horrible, I thought, to have that happen to anyone, especially a child. Then I heard that there wasn't any money to bury the child. I collected money for the funeral and gave it to the family. The child is at peace.

When I was eight, President George Bush named me the 779th Point of Light. I got to meet him in Biloxi, Mississippi, where he stopped off on his way back to Washington from the Republican National Convention in Houston. I told him that I was going to keep on helping people. He told me that I was special and that other boys and girls should think of ways to help people.

The next month, I heard about Hurricane Andrew and prayed that it would not hit the United States. After it did, television stories told of the people who lost their homes and everything in them. It made me very sad again and I wanted to do something. Soon Andrew came to Louisiana! Many people were suffering not too far from me. I collected 1,648 pieces of clothing for the families. The Red Cross came to my house and took the boxes of clothes to the people.

So many people have made contributions to my projects that my grandmother suggested that I start a foundation. That way, people would get credit for giving money, food, and clothes. Many boys and girls and men and women have helped me, so I wanted them to get credit. My grandmother and a lawyer worked with me to start the Isis Johnson Foundation. Imagine someone my age with a foundation!

Helping needy people is hard work, but fun, also. I intend to continue in any way that I can. It takes a lot of your time, and you have to think of how to do your best for others. I would like to tell other children to do good things for others. When you help them, you feel good about yourself.

The only problem I have had is that a few children act jealous. I tell them that anyone can do what I have done, and there are lots of problems in schools and towns, so they should get involved or start a special project of their own. When I'm older, I may be a doctor to help people.

What You Can Do

▶ Do some research to find people in your school and community who don't have enough food. How about in your state? Your nation? The world?

▶ Learn what action has been taken locally to help hungry people. If nothing or very little has been done, what can you do? Find out if any of the following groups are currently involved in helping the hungry in your community: churches, local restaurants, civic groups, your city council. How can you help these groups collect food for the needy?

▶ Many communities gather food for the hungry during holiday seasons. What can be done to be sure that hungry people get enough to eat all year long?

▶ Isis's efforts inspired many others to work hard to help hungry people. What can you do to inspire others in your community to be more giving?

▶ Isis started her very own foundation when she was eight years old. Research the types of foundations located in your community or state. How did they get started? What kinds of projects do they fund?

▶ Research the steps that are needed to start a foundation.

▶ Isis mentions that some children act jealous because of the things she has done. What can you do if your friends and classmates are jealous of your good deeds?

FIND OUT MORE, GET INVOLVED

Isis T. Johnson Foundation
1108 Leonidas Street
New Orleans, LA 70118

Provides information about the foundation's efforts to feed the hungry.

National Student Campaign Against Hunger & Homelessness
29 Temple Place
Boston, MA 02111

Lets students know how they can help solve the problems of hunger and homelessness.

Working Group on Domestic Hunger & Poverty
c/o National Council of Churches
475 Riverside Drive, Room 572
New York, NY 10115

Provides information on a wide range of projects that focus on hunger and poverty in the United States.

Melva T. Johnson

STARTING A READING EPIDEMIC

MELVA T. JOHNSON *was born in New York City on April 22, 1980, but her roots are steeped in the Southlands of her father's birthplace in Norfolk, Virginia, and her mother's in Rowland, North Carolina. Almost every summer, Melva returns to the South to visit her grandparents, aunts, cousins, an older sister, and scores of other relatives. Melva's relatives remind her that she is part of a wonderful family heritage that extends back through time. They also remind her that she has much to discover about life and other people.*

People in Melva's family love to read, and she inherited that joy from them. When she was a little girl, her relatives read her stories over and over again. Sometimes, they told her stories about things that had happened to them when they were children. These tales stirred Melva's imagination. Out of sheer curiosity, she learned to read when she was very young.

Through stories from her family and in her books, Melva heard and read about the world. When she was nine years old, she actually saw part of the world when she traveled to twelve cities in Egypt on a three-week vacation with her aunt. Melva visited ancient tombs, temples, and museums, took boat rides up the Nile, walked in the villages, and played with the children there. Her trip was a dream fulfilled.

Melva is in seventh grade and learning new things that will take her far. Some of her extracurricular activities include camping, swimming, dance lessons, and gymnastics. One of her exciting new ventures of 1992 was participating in the Girl Scouts Scholars program at Teachers College, Columbia University. In January 1993, Melva had the wonderful privilege of performing with other Girl Scouts at the dedication ceremony for the new office of the Girl Scouts of the U.S.A.

Melva believes that all these activities will help her make some exciting career choices. For now, she thinks about going into either law or medicine. The business end of the entertainment industry also interests her.

I BELONG TO A GIRL SCOUT TROOP THAT IS sponsored by a church in Jamaica, Queens, New York, and I noticed that a lot of the girls in my troop did not read very much. Whenever I talked about a good book that I had just finished, no one in my troop wanted to discuss it with me. That bothered me because part of the fun of reading is to bounce around ideas and opinions with your friends about the books you read.

I have a lot of books in my personal library at home that I have read and enjoyed. I thought it might be a good idea to encourage the Girl Scouts in my troop to discover the joy of reading as I had. I also wanted to earn Girl Scout badges and needed a project to work on. After talking it over with my troop leader, I decided to start a Girl Scout lending library.

I began by going through my library at home and pulling out the books that had won special awards, such as the Caldecott and Newbery medals. I decided to make a special category in the lending library for these books. To find out how these awards began and what they stood for, I did some research at the main branch of my public library. This information was not only for myself, but also for the girls in my troop. I wanted them to learn about these special book categories, too.

Back to my shelves at home, I continued to pull out books to add to the lending library. Soon, books covered my bed and spilled over on the floor. My aunt and I counted 210 of them.

Then we went out to the garage where we found a cart with wheels that was a perfect place to hold the stacks of books. The cart had a large top section as well as a section underneath into which all the books would fit quite nicely. Before I used it, however, my cousin and I dusted away the cobwebs, hosed down the shelves, replaced a few screws, and oiled the squeaky wheels. Now the cart was ready to roll and looked like new. My aunt and I loaded the cart and the books into the back of our old station wagon for the journey to our Girl Scout meeting room. The preparation time for all of this took about two weeks, but I knew it was time well spent.

What an exciting Girl Scout meeting it was that evening! We arranged all the books in the cart and tied a yellow ribbon around it. Our troop had a ribbon-cutting ceremony and officially announced the grand opening of the lending library. I took photographs and set up the sign-out sheets. Almost every girl selected several books to take home and read. To top it off, I received my first Girl Scout badge.

I created the lending library when I was 12. Since that time, I have earned 14 more badges in several other areas, including dance, theater, folk art, and music. I also received a U.S. Savings Bond by winning the read-a-thon at my school; I did that by reading over 100 books. Several of my classmates who did not participate that year told me that next time they would give me a run for my money. I like

Melva T. Johnson, second from left, shares her love of reading with members of her Girl Scout troop

that! It's a chance to inspire others to look at some of the things I do. That makes me feel so good inside.

I am still learning about leadership and there is so much more to know, but my advice to students is to concentrate your abilities and efforts on things you really enjoy doing. Start out by doing things close to home. There is much to be said about looking right in your own backyard for opportunities to help people. You can get a lot of support from people who know you. They can inspire you to act on things you have thought about. Once you begin a project, you can inspire others to do likewise. Try not to be sidetracked by being perfect—there is no such thing. Just do your best and learn from your mistakes.

Many times, just watching you in action or talking about what you have done will start others thinking about what they can do. Leadership is contagious. It moves from person to person; you can be the person who starts the epidemic. You will be amazed at how you can make a difference in ways that you never even thought about.

WHAT YOU CAN DO

▶ Find out if there are people in your school and community who do not read much or who do not have access to a variety of books. How could you organize a lending library for these people? What groups or resources could you contact to ask for donations of new or used books?

▶ Identify the groups of people in your community who don't know how to read or who can't read. Some examples are very young children, illiterate adults, and the visually impaired. How can you get organized to help people learn how to read?

▶ Write a city ordinance that asks every adult who can read to spend at least one hour per week with someone who can't read. Present your idea to the city council.

FIND OUT MORE, GET INVOLVED

Barbara Bush Foundation for Family Literacy
1002 Wisconsin Avenue, NW
Washington, DC 20007

Provides information on how to work with families to bring about literacy.

Book-It
Pizza Hut
National Reading Incentive Program
P.O. Box 2999
Wichita, KS 67201

Has information on a national program to increase children's interest in reading.

Laubach Literacy Action
Box 131, 1320 Jamesville Avenue
Syracuse, NY 13210

Supplies information on adult illiteracy and the Laubach approach to reading.

Reading Is Fundamental
600 Maryland Avenue, SW
Washington, DC 20024

Offers information on a school-based reading program for school-age students.

Julie Briley

SAVING THE BLUEBIRDS WHILE BEAUTIFYING THE PARKS

JULIE BRILEY'S *home is in Longview, Texas, where she lives with her mom and dad, Janine and Steven, and her two brothers, John and William. Julie's hobbies include working with her Camp Fire group, reading, drawing, and playing with her cat, Fluffy. She is an active person who enjoys piano lessons, gymnastics, and singing in the church choir. She also likes watching her brothers play baseball, soccer, and basketball.*

Julie attends Foster Middle School, where she is in the magnet program for gifted students. The events described below took place when she was a student at Hudson P.E.P. Elementary School, a magnet school with planned enrichment programs. She wrote about this project on behalf of her Camp Fire group.

$\mathcal{I}$F SIX YEARS AGO SOMEONE HAD TOLD ME that I would be invited to give a program for one of the largest rotary clubs in East Texas, be honored in the state Senate, and receive state and national awards for a service project, I would have called them crazy. But that and more has happened to me in the last few years of my life. Now that I am in middle school, I look back on my achievements and marvel at how they all happened.

It all began when I was in first grade. My Camp Fire group, the Bubbly Bluebirds, learned of a national effort to save the Eastern Bluebirds of East Texas. We also discovered that we could earn a Camp Fire badge by doing a project titled "Save the Bluebirds," described in Camp Fire's *Outdoor Handbook*. Our Camp Fire leaders read the badge requirements and decided that my group of 12 Bluebirds was mature enough to establish a bluebird sanctuary and maintain it for the life of the group. My leaders chose this project because it provided a way to save the bluebirds, improve our community, and teach leadership within my group.

My leaders asked the City of Longview Parks and Leisure Services (PALS) for permission to create a bluebird sanctuary in Guthrie Parkway. Permission was granted. A bluebird specialist taught us what we could do to help save the bluebirds. He helped us choose a trail that looked like a good site for our sanctuary. He also helped us and our parents put up boxes for bluebird nests.

The first year, only a chickadee built its nest in our boxes. "What went wrong?" we asked ourselves. We had followed all of the blue-bird specialist's instructions, but we had no bluebirds. We knew that bluebirds need water, nesting sites, food, and shelter. We had water in the stream that ran next to our trail. We had built nesting sites on our bluebird trail. What was missing? We decided our trail needed more winter food and more shelters.

We thought about giving up the project, but two things hap-pened. First, we won a national award and $100 in prize money from the fifteenth annual "Colgate's Youth for America" campaign for our project, "Bluebirds Save Bluebirds." Second, we developed a plan to improve the habitat of the bluebirds along our trail.

Julie Briley, **center, helps plant a tree during an Earth Day Celebration**

My mom (one of our leaders) presented our plan to Leadership Longview, a leadership training program for adults. Her class agreed to help us develop the steps needed to carry out our plan. The response from Leadership Longview encouraged us to continue our project.

Our specialist had taught us that bluebirds eat insects in the spring, summer, and fall, but they eat small berries in the winter when insect populations are low. Dogwood trees produce small red berries that bluebirds like, in addition to producing beautiful flowers in the spring. A landscape architect prepared a plan for our project that included dogwood trees. The superintendent of PALS approved the park layout.

We invited others to join our efforts to develop a pedestrian/ bluebird trail with dogwood trees in Guthrie Parkway. We let the community know about our "Save the Bluebirds and Beautify the Parks" project through the city newspaper, word of mouth, and the club newsletters of Camp Fire, Longview Chamber of Commerce, and Longview Senior Citizens. We included information about our project in registration mail-outs to youth groups. We wrote letters requesting funding from civic groups and handed out information from booths at community bazaars. We made formal presentations to the Longview Beautification Association, Boy Scout Roundtable,

Longview Nature Study Group, Greggton Rotary, and other local organizations.

We asked individuals, civic clubs, and businesses to sponsor a tree for a child to plant in the park. Each tree sponsor received a certificate of appreciation and we tagged a name onto the appropriate tree. We combined our "Save the Bluebirds" campaign with an Arbor Day Celebration and invited others from Camp Fire, Boy Scouts, Cub Scouts, Girl Scouts, senior citizens, and PALS to plant trees with us. Each participant received an Arbor Day Award and tagged a tree with his or her group's name.

It took two years to add trees to the landscaping plan. The third year we organized another Arbor Day Celebration to replace trees that had died.

The City of Longview Parks Department was so pleased with the Save the Bluebirds/Arbor Day Celebrations that it nominated the project for the Texas Urban Forestry Award (youth category). We were all surprised and delighted when we found out we had won.

Our Camp Fire group missed a day of school and traveled to Austin, Texas, to accept the award from the Texas Forest Service and the Texas Urban Forestry Council. While we were in Austin, a state senator introduced us to his colleagues on the floor of the Senate. He and a state representative honored our project by writing resolutions for permanent record in the Senate and the House of Representatives.

Since that time, our project has won awards and prizes from Keep Texas Beautiful, Incorporated, Keep America Beautiful, Incorporated, and the Environmental Protection Agency (EPA)-Region 6. Our group traveled to Houston and El Paso to accept some of these awards. The Texas Forest Service nominated our project for a National Arbor Day Foundation National Award.

We have had many exciting moments with the work of this project and the awards it has won. But we have also had many disappointments. Trees and nesting boxes are targets of vandalism. We raised the money to replant almost 70 trees that were damaged due to theft, vandalism, drought, heavy rains, weed-eaters, lawn mowers, and bad stock. The people who walk in the park are quick to criticize, but slow to help. Many times people ask, "Why don't they do something?" My question is: "Who are 'they'?"

It seems as if we have been checking bluebird boxes forever and, in the first five years of our project, only five bluebird nests (with eggs) have been built in our boxes. Helping nature is slow work. Our first bluebird nest with eggs was built in the project's third year, but the eggs were vandalized three days before they were to hatch. The second and third bluebird nests with eggs were built in the project's fourth year. Four bluebirds fledged from the second nest. The one-day-old chicks in the third nest were eaten by fire ants. The fifth year, we learned to prevent fire ants from disturbing the nests by painting the poles with axle grease. That year, 12 bluebirds fledged from three nests. In the years to come, we look forward to seeing baby bluebirds hatch again.

The leadership training we've had through Camp Fire has prepared my group to take the first steps to lead the project ourselves. We now have a committee and a chairperson who organize the project each year. It makes me proud that we are continuing to help save the bluebirds. Working on this project, I have learned a lot about nature. Things are more complicated than they seem at first.

Our project has affected not only my Camp Fire group, but other people in the community, state, and nation. Some contributed money or donated their time, labor, or expertise. Some even copied our project by organizing similar projects locally and nationally.

My mother signed me up in Camp Fire to improve my social skills. I have improved those skills, but have learned something much more important. You don't have to be important to do important things.

WHAT YOU CAN DO

▶ Find out about birds or other animals native to your area that are threatened or endangered. How could you provide a sanctuary for these animals? What local groups would you need to contact for help?

▶ Contact the garden clubs in your state and town. Some of them may have already started bird projects and would welcome your help. They could also assist you in starting a project of your own.

▶ Evaluate the parks in your community. Think about how they look and the kinds of activities you can do in them. What is needed to make your local parks more inviting? Find out what office is responsible for overseeing the use and beautification of local parks.

▶ Conduct a survey in your school or community to determine what people would like to have in local parks. Would they like more trees and wildlife? More tables and benches? More play equipment? Better litter control? A jogging trail? Using the results of the survey, think about how you can initiate a plan to make better use of local parks.

▶ Julie and her Camp Fire group volunteered much of their time to create a bluebird sanctuary. It's hard to save endangered and threatened wildlife when theft, vandalism, people's carelessness, and natural causes interfere. Do you think Julie's efforts were worth it? Are you willing to make a similar commitment? What if Julie's successful nests had held the last bluebirds on Earth?

FIND OUT MORE, GET INVOLVED

Camp Fire, Incorporated
4601 Madison Avenue
Kansas City, MO 64112-1278

This organization encourages self-reliance and good citizenship and will send information on its activities.

National Arbor Day Foundation
100 Arbor Avenue
Nebraska City, NE 68410

Will send free seedlings and information on planting trees.

National Audubon Society
950 Third Avenue
New York, NY 10022

Provides information on environmental issues.

Sierra Club
730 Polk Street
San Francisco, CA 94109

Offers information on the environment and related issues.

Touch America Program
U.S. Forest Service
P.O. Box 96090
Washington, DC 20090

Shares information on how to volunteer for conservation programs.

U.S. Field and Wildlife Service
Department of the Interior
18th and C Streets, NW
Washington, DC 20240

Has information on endangered species.

Carolyn Yagle

HELPING LATCHKEY CHILDREN

On a glorious spring morning in 1986, 11-year-old
CAROLYN YAGLE fulfilled a challenge—helping and
working with others in her hometown of Morgantown, West
Virginia. But it was not a one-time victory. The challenge —
proposed, accepted, and achieved on that day—continues to
be part of Carolyn's life.

Carolyn's challenge, a social studies project titled
"Latchkey Kids: How Can Society Help Them?" which she
and her partner created, won first place in a West Virginia
state competition on that spring day. Carolyn tells the
following story of her and her partner's research and hard
work from her perspective. Since the project was completed,
Carolyn has continued to use the research skills, study habits,
and compassion toward others that she gained while working
on the project.

Today, as a high school student, Carolyn interacts with
peers and teachers throughout the day—in class discussions,
cross-country running practice, band rehearsal, Peer Helpers,

drama classes, and church activities. Because of her many leadership and scholarship interests, Carolyn has been inducted into the West Virginia Honor Roll and the West Virginia Governor's Honor Academy. She also has been appointed president of her school's National Honor Society. An active, positive voice is one of Carolyn's assets. "Don't be afraid to ask questions" is one motto she learned from her friends, teachers, and parents. Each day, Carolyn knows she can face her challenges with control, helpful suggestions, and a smile.

Walking down Old Cabin Road, Kathleen kicked the colorful leaves to the sidewalk edges. Her friends, yelling from the windows of a passing school bus, reminded her of an afternoon game of tag. She nodded and waved as the yellow vehicle turned the corner. Skipping on the driveway, the fourth-grader made it to the side door and reached into her backpack to extract a key. Mrs. Harrow, hearing the shuffling and whistling, pulled back the lace curtains to see that her next-door neighbor had once again made it safely home.

Kathleen unlocked the side door and entered the kitchen. Realizing her stomach was growling, she shed her book bag, coat, the gloves her mother had told her to wear that morning, and tennis shoes. The freezer held ice cream, a treat that would satisfy her until dinner. As she stood up on the chair to reach into the icy compart-ment, her face and thoughts were stung by the cold air. Kathleen had no one to help her fix a sundae and no one to tell about the perfect score she had received on her social studies test.

$\mathcal{L}$IKE MILLIONS OF OTHER STUDENTS WHO come home every day to an empty house, Kathleen and I are latchkey children. As a high school junior, I am busy with school work, sports, and clubs; I sometimes return home at the same time or even later than my parents.

However, when my latchkey days began in the sixth grade, I walked into a quiet home every day at 4:00 p.m. Luckily, I felt comfortable being home alone; years of Girl Scouts and wise baby-sitters had taught me safety tips. More frightening to me was knowing that many school-aged children in the United States were not as fortunate. There are millions of latchkey children in this country today; thousands are able to reach help in seconds by dialing 911. Surprisingly, this resource is not available to every community; it wasn't in ours. At age 11, I wanted to make a change.

When I became a sixth-grader, I began my third year in the Extended Studies Program (ESP). Every Friday, I explored our school's library as a student in the class. For this opportunity, each student (or a pair of students) was required to complete an Independent Study Project by spring. Although I didn't know it at the time, a friend and I were about to start nine months of work and dedication that would result in a better community.

It wasn't a dark and stormy night but a crisp September morning when we began to search for an idea. Seated with our teacher, my fifth-grade partner and I brainstormed for an ESP project that we could also enter in the county's Social Studies Fair. Games, gambling, psychology, and sociology were our first ideas. The last topic mentioned—latchkey children—intrigued us the most. Not only could we study written materials, but we could also study people. Over the next few months, we researched this topic in two local libraries and produced valuable, riveting information. Together, we produced graphs and text with the school's and my partner's computers.

We discovered that many large American cities promote latchkey programs, and we thought about what we could do to help latchkey children in our community. A vital consideration, however, was to produce a program helpful to area residents. Leaders must learn to recognize needs and make decisions to accommodate many types of people. Our adventure began with surveying hundreds of second-, fourth-, and sixth-graders in a variety of neighborhoods. In this survey, we uncovered astonishing facts. We found out that many children come home to empty houses after school. Some are home alone for long periods of time. Brainstorming was again required to generate a plan that we could put into action.

We thought that computerizing our results in a presentable, convincing fashion would help our goal become more manageable. Winter came, and we screamed not for a snow day but for electricity. We learned that using a computer during a snowstorm is not wise—especially when the power goes out. As the white flakes fell, so did a lot of our data—into oblivion. A day's work was lost, but, calmly, we decided to design our display using attractive colors until the power was restored.

My partner and I wanted to offer after-school help to the many latchkey children in our area. We decided to put together a brochure for these students. The brochure would give suggestions on how to be safe, including calling a neighbor for help, and activities to do. It would also explain how to use the 911 emergency number. Of course, that meant that our community had to have 911 service. That would be the next part of our project.

Carolyn Yagle

With our project outline complete, the next step was to find a community leader we could work with. Mrs. Bucklew, the wife of the local university's president and a former Montana 911 employee, was a professional spokesperson with many abilities that enhanced our project. An afternoon interview with Mrs. Bucklew allowed us to express our concerns to an adult. Knowing we were worried about the safety of others, Mrs. Bucklew invited my friend and me to become members of her group that was petitioning to provide our county with a 911 program.

Enthusiasm thrived! We added the petition for a 911 number to our project. After weeks of preparation, we were eager to persuade the county commissioners and a room full of citizens that the new 911 plan would be worthwhile and necessary. Our jitters were overwhelming, for we were the only school-aged children there. We pointed out that if a child who was home alone got into a dangerous situation, he or she might not have any way to contact emergency help. We carefully outlined the proposal for a 911 number; we had no intention of giving up.

The public was impressed. Nevertheless, opposition groups appeared. In order to make 911 available, the phone company would require citizens to pay an extra phone charge each month. Some individuals, especially senior citizens, complained about the charge. My partner and I were not willing to return to the classroom and forget our goals, however. We were determined to succeed. Eventually, with the support of many community groups, our area received the 911 service.

To continue with our original project, we wrote two plays and designed a brochure called "When You're Home Alone: A Latchkey's Guide to the After-School Life." We also created a large poster and planned an oral presentation, which included a taped interview with Mrs. Bucklew.

April arrived. We entered our latchkey children project in a county social studies competition and competed against other sociology projects, which ranged from a study of the elderly to the effects of Agent Orange. We were compelled to do our finest, which meant poise and good communication and organization were essential. Our hard work paid off. We won first prize at the county level.

After we received first prize, my parents, my partner's sister, and her parents drove us to southern West Virginia for the next competition level. They took us to dinner Friday night, stayed with us in the motel, arranged a quick breakfast, and dropped us off at the civic center by 7:30 a.m. on Saturday. Rehearsing our speech one more time helped us to survive the first and second round of judging. We advanced to the final round. We were convinced we could achieve the best—helping others—if we worked together.

Our persistence was rewarded; it was amazing grace. As we heard our names announced as first-place winners, I recollected some of our project's most memorable experiences. Although it had been a challenge to conduct research and to maintain excellent grades at the same time, we had done it.

The many skills I utilized when interviewing adults or advocating our cause evolved into confidence and the desire to help and share with others. Leadership does not have to be confined within a school organization; I recommend that others become involved in the community.

The most worthwhile experience I gained from this project was learning the process involved in making a change. Unfamiliar agencies and public officials are now approachable. Because I confronted a city at age 11, I now find at age 16 that presentations are less frightening. I think people need to learn that the key to any undertaking is devotion and true interest. My partner and I were no exception. Encountering criticism has taught me to show persistence and courage in intimidating situations. Being prepared for sacrifice and knowing how to face adversity are qualities of effective leaders.

Brainstorming to identify interests and goals is an excellent starting point. Realistically, the greatest investment is not materials but time. An effective result deserves or requires thoroughness and determination.

A local associate minister preaching to a congregation said, "We make a living with what we get; we make a life with what we give." As an officer in two clubs, band member, baby-sitter, and volunteer in church activities and at the local public television station, I interact with many unique individuals. This involvement has enabled me to look forward to helping others, whether silently or in the limelight, in the future.

The bowl and the spoon were in the dishwasher. It would be two more hours before Kathleen's parents would come home. Kathleen planned to start an art project, but she didn't feel like being creative by herself.

She picked up the phone and dialed her next-door neighbor.

"Good afternoon, Mrs. Harrow. How have you been today?" Kathleen asked. "Me? Just great! I received the highest grade in the class on my social studies test. Sure, I'll be right over. I was going to do an art project. Yes, I'd love to do one together."

WHAT YOU CAN DO

▶ Are there any programs for latchkey children in your community? If there are, find out how you can help. If no project exists, find out if one is needed. How could you determine the number of latchkey children in your community? How could you reach the parents of latchkey children in order to determine their needs? Could you contact parent-teacher associations? Advertise in the local newspapers or on local radio and TV stations?

▶ The 911 emergency service allows people to reach help in seconds. Does your community offer this service? If so, design a plan to educate all young, preschool, and elementary children about the use of 911. If not, initiate a campaign to bring 911 service to your area.

▶ Find out other things latchkey children need besides access to emergency care. Do they need companionship? Supervision? Things to do besides watch TV? Think about programs for latchkey children you could start to meet these needs, such as after-school enrichment programs. As Carolyn suggested, brainstorm your interests and goals in leadership. Put them in priority order and get started.

FIND OUT MORE, GET INVOLVED

National Community Education Association
119 North Payne Street
Alexandria, VA 22314

Has information on community education for every citizen.

National Congress of Parents and Teachers Association (PTA)
700 North Rush Street
Chicago, IL 60611

Provides information on how parents and teachers can join together to help children and schools.

National Education Association
120 116th Street, NW
Washington, DC 20036

Write to this association to find out about the teaching profession and many educational projects.

Lee Palmer &
Janine Givens

EQUAL ACCESS
TO LIBRARY MATERIALS

LEE PALMER *is an eighth-grade student at Brooks School*
in Lincoln, Massachusetts. After Boston's WBZ radio show
"Kid Company" interviewed her about the library petition, Lee
became a reporter for the weekly show, which is by and about
kids. She interviews people and writes and presents features
and book reviews. Lee enjoys writing and in 1992 she won an
honorable mention in a national writing contest for "The
Revolution," her story about cats. Lee plays basketball and
soccer on both school and town teams. She loves animals (the
Palmer family has six cats), is a vegetarian, and has taken
stands against dissection as a routine learning tool in
required school science classes. (She favors the many
alternatives to dissection now available.) She is also interested
in politics and debate.

JANINE GIVENS *is in the eighth grade at Doherty Middle School in Andover, Massachusetts. She lives in an old Victorian farmhouse with her parents and five younger sisters. Janine's day begins at 5:30 a.m. when she gets up to deliver one of the Boston newspapers. In school, Janine enjoys writing and art—in fact, her bedroom walls are covered with her art projects. Outside of school, she keeps busy doing homework, talking on the telephone, baby-sitting, getting together with friends, and participating in a local children's theater. Janine enjoys biking, camping, and walking in the woods near her home. Her hobbies are collecting cows and any materials connected with* The Phantom of the Opera.

$\mathcal{T}$HE ANDOVER, MASSACHUSETTS, MEMORIAL Hall Library had a policy that prevented children under grade seven from using the main floor of the library on their own. This policy was frustrating for us because the main floor consisted of the entire adult and young adult collections and the magazine and biography sections. As fifth-graders at South Elementary School in Andover, we were not supposed to be on the main floor. This policy was never publicly posted so most of Andover's residents did not know of its existence. We did not know of the policy, either, but several times we were asked to leave the main floor when we weren't sure why.

One time, we specifically remember being asked to leave the main floor. We were in the young adult section looking for books. A library monitor came up to us and asked our grade. When she found out that we were in the fifth grade, she asked us to go to the children's room. On our way downstairs to the children's room, we stopped in the biography section to look at some titles for our biography book report. After we had both found good books, the same monitor, who had apparently followed us, entered the room. The monitor was not pleased to find us and angrily told us again to go downstairs. After that experience, we were scared to go back to the library. Our parents were surprised to hear our story. They said we shouldn't feel scared to be in a library.

We wanted to find out ways to let the library know how we and other kids felt about the way we were treated in the library. Lee's mom told us that she had started an adults' petition asking the library to change its policy. We asked her if starting a children's petition would be a good idea. She thought it was a great idea and that same night we wrote one. Our petition stated:

"We the undersigned children of Andover feel that the Memorial Hall Library's policy concerning children below grade seven not being allowed on the main floor is unjust. We feel that this policy is unfair because it makes us feel unwelcome in the library. Also, not being allowed to use our own card throughout the library very much discourages us. We hope you take this petition into serious consideration and change the policy so that we may feel more welcome in our own library."

After getting permission from our school's principal, we asked the kids in school if they would read and sign our petition. In just two days, we collected over 150 signatures of third-, fourth-, and fifth-grade students. A few supportive teachers also signed our petition.

As we collected signatures, a lot of kids shared stories of their own frustrating experiences at the library. Some seventh-graders even came up to us and told us their stories. They said they were asked to leave the adult area even though they were supposedly allowed to be there. The library monitors sometimes didn't even ask kids their ages and assumed that if they were short they were too young. Many kids were not only insulted but humiliated, too.

In early June we presented the petition to the library. One thing was sure: We all wanted full use of the library.

In mid-June, Sarah Wunsch, an attorney at the Civil Liberties Union of Massachusetts, answered our cry for support and wrote a letter to the library asking that kids be allowed equal access. She did this because the library was violating children's First Amendment rights. We were thankful for the Civil Liberties Union's quick response to what we thought was an urgent issue. To this day, we are very grateful for their unwavering helpful attitude toward us.

On October 20, we attended the Massachusetts Civil Liberties Union's annual Bill of Rights dinner in Boston to hear Julian Bond give a special speech. In an introductory speech, John Roberts, the union's executive director, mentioned our concern and what we had done about it. We received a standing ovation.

On December 3, we delivered a speech about the library issue at a conference for youths ages 11 through 17 that was sponsored by the Massachusetts Civil Liberties Union Foundation's Bill of Rights Education Project. The conference explored the topic "What Would Life Be Like without the Bill of Rights?" Our speech was later published in a children's magazine.

In the weeks that followed, we wrote letters, talked on local radio stations, spoke with newspaper reporters, and appeared on Boston TV and radio stations. Finally, the library agreed that, for the

Janine Givens, left, and *Lee Palmer* with their petition

first time, Andover students would be allowed free access to all library areas and almost all materials, no matter what age, for a six-month trial period.

In six months, the trial period ended and the library's trustees voted on the issue of equal access to the library facility. The vote was 6 to 1 for the kids. This proved to us, and many others involved, that kids can change things with help and guidance from adults. We will continue to stand up for things that we know are wrong and advise other kids to do the same. If you believe in something strong enough, there are no limits to what you can do, even if you're a kid, because this is our world, too!

WHAT YOU CAN DO

▶ Find out your library's policy on who has access to its materials. Does your library restrict elementary school students from using some sections on their own? If so, compose an ordinance stating that everyone has an equal right to use library materials. Present the ordinance to your city council and place it in your library

▶ Are there policies in your school or community that seem unfair to you? If you feel strongly about making a change in your school, discuss your concerns with the principal. If you feel a change needs to be made in your community, set up an appointment to talk to your mayor or other local official.

▶ If you believe your rights have been violated, think about how you can present your case to adults. Petitions are often used as forceful documents. Find out the process for starting a petition and the best procedure for getting signatures.

▶ Have you ever violated the rights of another person, unintentionally or on purpose? Brainstorm a list of ways that people violate others' rights. What can you do to change these violations?

FIND OUT MORE, GET INVOLVED

American Civil Liberties Union
132 West 43rd Street
New York, NY 10036

This organization provides information on the rights of young people in and out of school.

National Collaboration for Youth
1319 F Street, NW, Suite 601
Washington, DC 20004

Offers information on agencies that use a variety of programs to serve young people.

Sydney Myddelton

THE SHOW MUST GO ON

The project described in this chapter opened many doors for 16-year-old SYDNEY MYDDELTON. For example, she was asked to direct her church's Christmas youth musical, which involved 40 young people, and she ran for student body president of her high school and won.

At Leon High School in Tallahassee, Florida, Sydney serves as chaplain of the Anchor Service Club. She is a member of the National Honor Society and the Fellowship of Christian Athletes. She also serves as the show coordinator on the local teen board for Gayfers Department Store. She has served three years on the Pride National Youth Team and two years as a trainer and consultant.

Sydney plans to pursue her education at the University of Georgia, where her parents and older brother and sister have attended. She hopes to major in communications, specifically in public relations.

$\mathcal{O}$N WEDNESDAY, MAY 15, 1991, I WAS informed of the devastating news that CAST, the Center for the Arts School of Theater, was closing due to a lack of revenue. CAST is a community nonprofit theater in Tallahassee that trains youth in voice, dance, and drama. It also presents young people with the opportunity to perform in actual shows or productions. I spent so many hours there that it had become like a second home. It represented everything I have ever wanted to do!

When I heard the news, I knew I couldn't let the theater close. I felt there must be something I could do to help it survive. I decided I would get the other kids involved. After all, they had a vested interest, also! A good friend of mine was just as concerned as I and was ready to take action. We put our heads together and decided to write a show expressing our feelings about CAST. It had become more than just a theater to us, it was actually like a family. We would do a show for the adults at CAST and any other people who were interested. Maybe it would stir their emotions and motivate them to support the efforts of CAST.

Now the real work began. My friend and I immediately started writing the show. Up until that point, I had never realized how hard a writer's job was. In order to write the show, we did a considerable amount of research. After completing the script, we gathered 20 kids who were involved in CAST and shared our interest in helping the organization. The vote was unanimous to proceed so we were off and running. We wrote up a rehearsal schedule, organized committees, and began rehearsals.

During the next two months, we overcame many obstacles. One of the most frustrating aspects during this project was the lack of commitment on the part of some kids. Despite that, after two-and-a-half months, the show was well-rehearsed and ready. During the time of rehearsing, we also had three fund-raisers going on. We sold candy and held a raffle with donated prizes, which worked very well. We had a garage sale, but unfortunately that idea bombed. The two successful fund-raisers allowed us to cover expenses such as music and costumes. As we were organizing the show, CAST directors

Sydney Myddelton, fourth from right, with members of CAST

found a location that the theater could use for free, so we didn't have to worry about raising money for rent.

On April 28, 1992, *Coming To Gather* was performed under lights on a bi-level stage. Two hundred people were present for our amateur production. It was a success! Many parents realized the love for CAST that the kids felt and the need to keep such a good thing going.

Despite our efforts, however, CAST did close. But a very strong bond among those who participated in the Center for the Arts School of Theater remains.

Coming To Gather was definitely the largest project I have attempted so far. It was an incredible amount of work and took a lot of time, but the reward was phenomenal. The payoff encouraged me to take more leadership positions. I would suggest that others take advantage of the opportunity to be a leader. The reward is awesome.

WHAT YOU CAN DO

▶ Examine your school or community for opportunities for creative expression through the arts. Look into the park district or local colleges and universities for theater, dance, art, and music programs. If these opportunities exist, find out if they are available to children from all socioeconomic backgrounds. If they aren't, what can you do to encourage these programs to offer their services to all kids?

▶ Think about how you might generate interest in theater, dance, art, and music programs in your school and community. Would you create posters to hang in store windows and on school boards? Advertise in the local newspaper? Write announcements to air on TV and radio stations? Present your idea at a parent-teacher association meeting?

▶ Brainstorm all the benefits of creative expression through theater, dance, art, and music. How could you convey these benefits to others? What resources are needed for such programs? What kinds of people are needed? Facilities? Money?

▶ In spite of Sydney's efforts, CAST was closed. Do you think that because of this, she got nothing out of her project? Think of something you have tried in your life that didn't work out in the way you had hoped. Make a list of the benefits you received from just trying.

FIND OUT MORE, GET INVOLVED

Creative Response
9502 Lee Highway, Suite B
Fairfax, VA 22031

Supplies information on cultural exchanges you can get involved in to bring about better world understanding.

International Thespian Society
3368 Central Parkway
Cincinnati, OH 45225

Sends out information on the theater and includes suggestions on how you can get involved in local productions.

Tri-M Music Honor Society
1902 Association Drive
Reston, VA 22091-1597

This organization emphasizes service through music. Write to Tri-M to find out how you and a teacher/adviser can start a chapter at your high school.

Joanne Buenzli & Christine Muchi

PAINTING WITH PATIENTS

JOANNE BUENZLI and CHRISTINE MUCHI are 16-year-old juniors at North Allegheny Senior High School in Wexford, Pennsylvania, a suburb of Pittsburgh. Joanne maintains a 3.9 GPA and participates in student council and school plays. Between going to school and working, Joanne usually doesn't have time to become involved in all the activities she would like. Christine plays field hockey on North Allegheny's team and has a 3.8 GPA. She hopes to continue developing the skills necessary to function and contribute as a leader in today's world.

The success of their leadership project described below encouraged the two young women to pursue another one. They collaborated on a workshop about stereotyping called "Stereotyping: Clear as Black and White." They presented the workshop to groups of students at a student council conference and to a group of Future Leaders at a Leadership Olympics.

$\mathcal{A}$T NORTH ALLEGHENY SENIOR HIGH School, we took a very enlightening course on leadership. Part of the course curriculum was to do a leadership project that involved leading other people in school, business, or the community.

We brainstormed for days and then came up with the idea of the century. We would raise some spirits and create a beautiful piece of artwork by working with children at the Children's Hospital of Pittsburgh. We would help the young patients design and paint a mural about the hospital. We hoped to help them realize all the things Children's Hospital does for them. We also wanted to keep the children busy and in high spirits, because we thought many of them would be nervous about staying in a hospital. Not only would we be doing our leadership project, but we would also be turning frowns into smiles. And that's exactly what we did.

We titled our project "Paintin' Patients" and wrote up a plan to submit to the hospital. In our plan, we proposed our idea of painting a mural, stated our goals, and described our leadership course. A few days later, the Director of Volunteers gave us the go-ahead. The Child Life Specialist at Children's Hospital also approved our plan.

When we arrived at Children's Hospital for our painting class, we learned that we'd be working in the Cardiology Clinic, instead of the General Clinic area as we had planned. The young patients in cardiology all had some sort of heart condition that needed treatment. We also learned that because of the change in the hospital schedule, we would only be working with seven kids. They were more than willing to paint, though, and we knew our project would serve as a diversion from their anxiety.

At first, it was difficult for the young children to grasp the concept of our mural. It was hard to convey the idea that we wanted them to paint people and things that were part of the hospital. We think that some patients felt uncomfortable showing their feelings and that it was easier for them to paint rainbow stripes. If we hadn't stood behind our idea, we would have lost patience right away.

By the end of the day, the kids had completed the mural. The finished painting had an outline of two children standing on a cloud. They held a banner with the name of the hospital on it. Inside the cloud, the patients had painted pictures showing how they felt about the hospital. The hospital staff hung up our mural for everyone to enjoy.

The strengths of our project were patience and organization. We began with a positive attitude and tried to "energize" the children with our own enthusiasm. We also had a lot of confidence in our project and stood behind it 100 percent. If we hadn't shown our patience and positive attitude, we wouldn't have completed this project as well as we had, since the children needed considerable guidance.

We learned a lot by doing this project and, if we were to do another one, we would make some changes. First, we'd try to encourage the children to paint original pictures instead of just painting one of the sections of our pre-drawn outline. Second, we would plan the space on our paper better. It was difficult for us to judge how much space was needed for imagination and how much space would let the children get out of control with the paint.

Throughout the project, we found it challenging to work with children and paint. There really was nothing we could have done when they got out of hand unless we had learned to tame six-year-olds, and if we could do that we wouldn't need to go to school . . . we would be millionaires.

Christine Muchi, right, and Joanne Buenzli, second from right, paint with Children's Hospital patients

If we were to repeat this project, we would also set stricter guidelines. Before we let the children start painting, we would sit them down and fully explain what we wanted to achieve. Then we would block off areas so one picture could be in each space. That way, we wouldn't have children painting on other children's pictures. We would allow freedom of expression and ask the children to really think about what they were painting. Another idea would be to get one or two other students to take pictures and help us take care of the paint table, smocks, and clean up.

We learned that it wasn't hard to get smiles out of the patients. Because each had basically come to terms with his or her heart problem, we learned more about what the hospital does for the children than the children did. We thought the children would be depressed about staying in the hospital, but almost all of them spoke of their condition matter-of-factly; they cheered us up as much or maybe more than we cheered them up. The young patients renewed our confidence in their generation by showing us how strong they were.

This project taught us that not all goals can be written or measured. The feeling of genuine happiness that these children radiated brought us greater satisfaction than any of the project's written goals.

Our advice to future leaders is don't be afraid to get out there and try things you've never done before; mistakes are inevitable for even the most experienced leader. We believe that leadership is an element of success that needs to be taught to today's young adults. *Carpe Diem*—Seize the Day—has become our motto.

WHAT YOU CAN DO

▶ Think about a project you could do to help young children in hospitals in your own town or city. Present your plan to the volunteer staff at a local hospital.

▶ Contact the hospital in your area and ask about volunteer programs that already exist. Does the hospital have a "Candy

Stripers" program you could join? What other hospital programs interest you?

▶ Joanne and Christine helped children create a mural to decorate the hospital walls. Brainstorm a list of places in your school or community that would benefit from beautification through the arts. Are there buildings or sections of town that could be enhanced by painted murals? Identify those most in need and design a plan of action for beautification. Who would you need to ask for permission to paint the mural? Who could help you? What companies could donate paint? How long would it take to complete the project?

FIND OUT MORE, GET INVOLVED

American Red Cross
Programs and Services Department
Youth Associate
431 18th Street, NW
Washington, DC 20006

Provides information on how you can become involved in Red Cross activities.

Close Up Foundation
1235 Jefferson Davis Highway
Arlington, VA 22202

Provides information on social responsibility projects and ways you can get involved.

Volunteers of America, Incorporated
3813 North Causeway Boulevard
Metairie, LA 70002

Will send information on how you can become a volunteer. Will also provide a list of projects that need volunteers.

Amy Schott

BRINGING A COMMUNITY TOGETHER

AMY SCHOTT, 19, *became interested in leadership in the sixth grade when she was elected to the student council. With help and encouragement from her advisers, she stayed active and held every office possible in both middle school and high school. She also held the office of vice president of the West Virginia Association of Student Councils.*

Amy grew up in a single-parent home in Gassaway, West Virginia, where she lived with her mother, who made education a top priority in their home. Her father was abusive and an alcoholic. Living without a father figure was one major obstacle Amy had to overcome in her life. However, she believes that the experience made her a stronger person and inspired her to pursue her dreams and make them a reality.

The success of the candlelight service described in this story gave Amy the confidence to press forward and set higher goals. Her leadership positions and awards have broadened her capabilities. In 1992, she became the first person in her family to attend college when she started classes at the

University of Utah in the pre-pharmacy program. In January 1993, she was invited to enroll in the honors program. Amy knows deep in her heart that she has the dedication, willingness, and experience to excel in college.

Amy believes success not only comes from hard work, but from honesty as well. She is organized and prioritizes goals; her strongest characteristic is having an optimistic attitude about life. According to Amy, being positive and open-minded when facing life's challenges and obstacles can unlock many doors. These qualities are also necessary to avoid crumbling under pressure.

IN AUGUST 1990, IRAQI TROOPS INVADED the small country of Kuwait in the Middle East. In response to that invasion, President George Bush ordered U.S. forces to Saudi Arabia, which borders Kuwait. President Bush told Iraqi officials that if they did not remove their troops by January 15, 1991, the United States would declare war.

In late 1990, as the president's deadline approached, tension mounted and the fear could be felt in my community of Gassaway. Many families had received word that their loved ones had gone or would soon be deployed to Saudi Arabia. My brother served in the U.S. Army and was stationed in Berlin, Germany, so I struggled with the same fears.

My community is small. We are like family. I felt there had to be some way to pull us together in this time of uncertainty. After several days of searching, I decided to organize a candlelight vigil in recognition of all the men and women serving in the armed forces. I shared this idea with my mother and she was excited about it; I enlisted her support and energy.

My first step was to map a course of action. I had to be well organized to tackle this project and make it successful. I decided to plan the vigil for a night in early December. I made an outline to follow and charged ahead. I contacted the mayor and asked for permission to host the event in front of the community building. He was more than happy to approve such an undertaking and enthusiastically pledged his and the town's support.

The next step was to plan a program for that night. After several rough drafts and piles of crumpled paper, I narrowed down the possibilities. I contacted the ministers and priests of the various denominations in the community and asked them to speak at the vigil. All accepted and were glad for the opportunity to give comfort and hope to the citizens. The youth choir from one of the churches agreed to sing a medley of songs.

I also wanted to include an event that all the citizens could participate in. Therefore, I asked everyone to bring a yellow ribbon with them to the vigil to place on the town Christmas tree. These ribbons would remain on the tree to remind passersby of the servicemen and women, at home and abroad, who had fought or were now serving to keep our country free. I also asked them to bring the names and addresses of these soldiers so that the information could be given out to anyone wishing to write to them.

Amy Schott ties a yellow ribbon on the town Christmas tree for her brother

Local newspapers, radio stations, and TV stations generously offered to do free advertising to promote the vigil. Once the advertising began, my phone rang off the hook. The local fire department volunteered to bring ladders to use in tying the ribbons onto the tree. The local florist donated candles. Families thanked me for letting them feel like they were doing something for their loved ones.

The night of the vigil—December 10, 1990—finally arrived. Outside the community building, I prepared a table with a large, round white candle; a United States flag; red, white, and blue streamers; and an enormous yellow ribbon. I readied another table with programs, paper, pencils, candles, extra yellow ribbons, and of course, my brother's address. I made sure the tables were under plenty of light. The only thing left now was to wait.

I began to question whether having 100 programs printed was presumptuous on my part. It was an extremely cold, crisp evening. Maybe, I thought, it was too cold for people to come. As I stood and observed with great anxiety, the crowd gathered. As the youth choir began to sing, the area was filled as far as I could see. There had to be over 200 spectators holding their yellow ribbons and candles in their mitten-covered hands.

With tears streaming down their faces, mothers, fathers, grandparents, sisters, and brothers placed ribbons with the names of their loved ones on the tree. I, too, swallowed the lump in my throat, wiped my eyes, and placed my brother's ribbon on the tree.

As we sang, listened, and prayed together that night, I realized that our community had truly become one. In the glow of candlelight, all my challenges, hard work, and dedication were rewarded. I knew I had made a difference, and the glow on my face was as bright as the brightest candle that night.

Looking back on my years in school, I recognized how much my leadership skills have grown. I am so grateful for the support of my advisers who saw my potential and encouraged me. I am thankful to all the adults in my life who gave me the opportunity to make decisions for myself. Thinking for myself has helped me to become a better leader.

I realize I have grown as a leader. I have developed confidence in myself and gained trust and respect from my peers. These skills will be permanent tools for me to utilize and develop as I face other challenges in my life.

I dare every student to face challenges and to set their goals high. You *can* make a difference in your school and community. You will become a more effective leader and fine-tune your leadership skills as you struggle to achieve the tasks set before you.

The sky is the limit if you believe in yourself. Believe in yourself and shoot for the stars. You never know what galaxy you might land in.

WHAT YOU CAN DO

▶   Identify situations in your school or community that cause unusual stress or strain. Conduct a survey to determine negative and positive situations. Think about how you could map a course of action to alleviate these negative situations and bring the school or community together. What problem-solving strategies could you use?

▶   Every school and community has at least one reason to celebrate its accomplishments. Brainstorm a list of positive accomplishments or reasons to celebrate. Develop a plan to do so.

▶   Although Amy proved you don't have to be elected to be a leader, holding elected positions in school organizations had given her confidence. Find out the elected positions that exist in your school. Which positions interest you? How could you go about seeking an elected position? What special responsibilities would this position involve?

FIND OUT MORE, GET INVOLVED

BACM (Back America's Courageous Military)
5210 West 141st Street
Savage, MN 55378

This national organization collects and distributes information to help people who have friends and family serving in the military. This group also provides the names and addresses of servicemen and women working overseas.

USO Louisville Service Club
Pen Pal Program
13 Lee Terminal
Standiford Field
Louisville, KY 40209

The USO Pen Pal Program provides the names and addresses of servicemen and women working overseas. Contact the USO to find out how you can send letters and packages to people in the armed forces.

Andrea Simkins

OPERATION HOMELESS

Eighteen-year-old ANDREA SIMKINS, an only child, lives in Wilmington, Delaware, with her parents, Alan and Sandra Simkins. Andrea's father is a dentist and her mother is a teacher of grades four through six.

Andrea's interests include helping others. As a Big Sister in Concord High School's "To Be Friends" program, she visited with an at-risk elementary school fifth-grader once a week at the local elementary school. When the program was not implemented for her senior year, Andrea sought adult sponsorship and started her own program at the elementary school where her mother works. Because of the program's success, Andrea was named the national winner of the "Spirit of America" award sponsored by Clairol.

In addition, during her senior year Andrea was named an All-Star Cheerleader. She served as a "buddy" to a mentally disabled ten-year-old for the year, culminating in an All-Star football game in June that raised money for the Retarded Foundation.

Andrea was also president of Students Against Drunk Driving (SADD) and increased membership from 40 students to over 500 (out of a school population of 1,000). The group held monthly activities to raise awareness about wearing seat belts and about the dangers of drunk driving. On an unannounced police check one morning, police officers found that 94 percent of the students entering the school parking lot were wearing seat belts. Andrea's school had the state's highest percentage.

Since seventh grade, Andrea has volunteered, and was one of the first to recruit high school volunteers, for the Flower Market, a three-day charitable carnival benefiting children's agencies. Now, almost every high school in her county has a student volunteer group.

Andrea's other interests include creative writing, politics, traveling, cheerleading, and snow skiing. She has received numerous awards and is included in Who's Who among American High School Students.

In 1992, Andrea began attending Vanderbilt University in Nashville, Tennessee, where she hopes to go on to graduate school in law. She would eventually like to serve in local, state, and national government.

I WAS INSPIRED BY A NEWSPAPER ARTICLE about a 12-year-old boy who delivered sandwiches and hot chocolate to the homeless in Philadelphia. After investigating the situation in my own hometown of Wilmington, I was amazed to discover the plight of homeless families with small children, many of whom lived in cars.

Andrea Simkins, right, with her "buddy," Leanne Evans, who is the Delaware All-Star child for the Retarded Foundation, and Larry Griffin, Delaware's All-Star football player

When I was a sophomore at Concord High School, I began "Operation Homeless" in conjunction with the annual canned food drive for the needy. My social studies teacher, who was active in Habitat for Humanity, agreed to sponsor my project. I also organized a group of students to help me.

We made posters announcing a clothing drive for the homeless and put them up around school. We wrote announcements about how to donate clothing and read them over the PA system.

The students at my school responded generously. Within two months, they had donated blankets, sleeping bags, winter coats, and other clothes including hats, scarves, and gloves in children's sizes. All items received were dry-cleaned, free of charge. (A local dry cleaner donated the service.) We delivered them, in time for the winter months, to a charitable organization. The organization distributed the items to the homeless families in Wilmington.

After two successful seasons, Operation Homeless, of which I am chairperson, was incorporated into Concord High's chapter of the National Honor Society. The Honor Society sponsors this project and student volunteers continue the organization's work.

My work with the homeless did not stop with the annual drive, however. The Ministry of Caring, Wilmington Chapter, contacted me and asked if Concord High students would get involved with the chapter's newly established day care center for children of homeless working parents. I contacted school groups to see if they were interested in helping with this worthy cause. I also hope to continue volunteering for similar groups while I attend college.

My advice to students everywhere is to look around your community and determine its needs. By becoming involved, you will reap the rewards of satisfaction and accomplishment in helping other people.

WHAT YOU CAN DO

▶ Plan your own clothing drive. Who could you ask for clothing donations? How would you let people know about the event? Is there a charitable organization in your community that accepts clothing for homeless people? If there is, find out where to drop off the clothing you collect. If there is no organization, find out how you could get the donated clothing to homeless people.

▶ In almost any community in the nation, people are homeless. What do you think are the underlying problems creating homeless-ness? Find out if your community is addressing these problems. If it isn't, how could you attract attention to the problems? Is a food drive needed for the homeless in your community?

▶ Find out who cares for homeless children in your community. Think about helping out by developing after-school programs for these children. How about organizing adult volunteers to care for preschool homeless children during the day?

▶ Think about local businesses and industries you could approach to ask about job opportunities for homeless adults.

FIND OUT MORE, GET INVOLVED

Habitat for Humanity International
121 Habitat Street
Americus, GA 31709

Write to this organization to find out how others have provided shelter for the homeless and ways you can help.

National Coalition for the Homeless
1621 Connecticut Avenue, NW, No. 400
Washington, DC 20009

Will send information on how you can help solve the homelessness problem.

Katie Christie

EMPOWERING OTHERS
TO MAKE A CHANGE

Twenty-one-year-old KATIE CHRISTIE *of Miami, Florida,
has been involved in the arts her whole life. Play rehearsals,
dance lessons, and singing practice once took up all of her free
time. While attending the New World School of the Arts,
Katie realized that although she loved being on stage, she
wanted to do something about all the horrible things,
including discrimination and prejudice, she saw on the news.*

*Born of mixed-race parentage and adopted as a newborn
by a Greek-Jewish couple, Katie was confused about her racial
identity. She grew up with a deep sensitivity about what it is
to be different. Katie decided to commit her life to the pursuit
of world peace and the breaking down of racial and ethnic
barriers.*

*Katie now attends Miami-Dade Community College and
works with the Tactual Speech Project for Hearing Impaired
Children at the University of Miami.*

In 1988, I heard about Creative Response (formerly called the Peace Child Foundation). That program, I felt, would help me convey my message of peace through the arts. Creative Response made my dream a reality when they selected me to be a part of their international youth exchange program. In the summer of 1988, I traveled to Latvia, then part of the Soviet Union, and learned that I could make a difference and spread my message the best way I knew how, through musical theater.

Upon returning from my trip, I organized Voices United (formerly called Peace Child Miami). It became one of the many chapters of Creative Response across the United States. Each year, Voices United would put on productions that emphasized unity among races and addressed social problems. I would act as director and audition cast members. I convinced my father and mother that this was a worthy project, and they agreed to help me begin my crusade. After many difficult hours of planning and often discouraging meetings, I overcame the prejudices that go along with being a young woman trying to accomplish something in today's world.

Following auditions in January of 1989, I assembled a cast of 60 kids. The cast members and I discussed our feelings about nuclear war and wrote a script that conveyed our message of nonviolent conflict resolution. Every Saturday for five months, we worked on our production, which related to the Soviet Union and United States's peaceful resolution.

In 1990, my chapter and I turned our energies to the concept of solving our own community's problems. We put together a production called City at Peace, a show that dealt with Miami's problems of drugs, violence, and racial tension. My main goal was to bring kids together from diverse and conflicting communities and help them realize that if we joined forces, we could make a difference. And that is exactly what happened.

I pulled together a new group of 100 kids to work on the new show. When the cast members arrived for the first rehearsal, everyone sat down in groups that they were comfortable in (blacks sat with blacks, whites with whites, and Hispanics with Hispanics). Through games and exercises, I mixed up the group. All of a sudden, everyone became more comfortable with people they had something in common with regardless of their ethnic background. That's what it's all about! We got down to business and the real action took place each Saturday at our rehearsals.

The show was our way of sharing our message with the rest of the city. At the end of our *City at Peace* production, those 100 kids left knowing what they had to do to make a difference in their families, schools, and communities. The following year, our chapter produced another *City at Peace* show with 100 new kids.

After this show, I began to work with the Tactual Speech Project for Hearing Impaired Children at the University of Miami. Voices United did a show called *Kids for Kids* to raise money for this program. The cast, made up of hearing and hearing-impaired children, created a script that dealt with the stigma of being disabled. Once again, the most inspiring aspect of this production was not the actual play, but the process. The kids in this production learned what it was like to be disabled and addressed the misconceptions often associated with disabilities. This experience was a tremendously moving one that inspired me to pursue a degree in special education.

In the summer of 1991, Creative Response asked me to apply my local directing experience abroad. I returned to the former Soviet Union as the artistic director on a Creative Response exchange

**Katie
Christie**

program, similar to the one I had been part of in the summer of 1988. This program brought 15 American and 15 Soviet kids together to write a show about their concerns. Working in two languages in a foreign country was an immense challenge for me. Those obstacles, however, slowly disappeared as we all grew closer together to achieve our goal.

The next year, our local chapter focused on the family with our new production, *Be a Family*. The idea behind this production was to promote communication, build understanding, and create a forum to develop solutions to the complex problems facing our families. The cast of more than 100 actors, singers, and dancers once again represented a mixture of black, white, and Hispanic kids (ages 5 to 20). Gathering material for this show was more difficult than with the others because many of the kids were extremely sensitive about their families. What made this show special was the fact that everyone has a family, no matter what shape or size, and everyone can relate to family problems. The script dealt with child abuse, teen pregnancy, drugs in the family, interracial families, and divorce. Our major idea behind the show was that we need to get back to the basics and work on our families.

In July of 1992, I traveled to South Africa on another Creative Response exchange program. This project brought together American kids—black, white, and Hispanic—with black, Indian, and Afrikaner kids from the host country. The show was the first of its kind in South Africa, and an inspirational experience for me. I was impressed by the way the South Africans have taken up the struggle to make change, and compared their actions to the passivity I feel in the United States.

All of these experiences have changed my life and the lives of the other children involved. The main idea behind my work is to empower others just as Creative Response has empowered me. There is so much work to be done in America and in the rest of the world, and that work has everyone's name on it. I feel that anyone can be a leader, and the first step is taking charge of your own life.

WHAT YOU CAN DO

▶ Katie used her strengths in the arts to bring people of all types together. What are your strengths? How could you use them to make a positive contribution to your world?

▶ Katie turned her feelings of being different into one of her biggest assets as a leader. Is there any way in which you feel different or confused about who you are? Think of ways to build on these feelings and turn them into strengths.

▶ The Creative Response productions tackled issues of racial prejudices, drugs, violence, family communication, child abuse, teen pregnancy, divorce, and interracial families. What special problems confront your school, community, and state? Conduct a survey to determine other people's perceptions of the most pressing issues. Decide how you might approach these issues in a positive way.

▶ Katie stresses the need to empower others toward the common good of all. As a leader, how can you best empower other people?

▶ Leadership begins with taking charge of your life, says Katie. How might you take charge of your life? Through goal setting and action toward those goals? Through organization and time management? Generate a list of areas in your life that need improvement. Start working on these areas today.

FIND OUT MORE, GET INVOLVED

Big Brothers/Big Sisters of America
230 North 13th Street
Philadelphia, PA 19107

Has information about projects you can join to help children deal with problems such as child abuse, drugs, and other social concerns.

Creative Response (formerly the Peace Child Foundation)
9502 Lee Highway, Suite B
Fairfax, VA 22031

Supplies information on cultural exchanges you can get involved in to bring about better world understanding.

National Volunteer Hotline
425 Second Street, NW
Washington, DC 20001

Will send information on how you can become a volunteer, along with a list of projects that need volunteers.

United Neighborhood Centers of America
4801 Massachusetts Avenue, NW
Washington, DC 20016

Offers information on improving the quality of life in local neighborhoods.

LEADERSHIP IN ACTION:
IN SCHOOL

You can find opportunities for school leadership in clubs,
organizations, and student government. Look around your
school. Are there conditions you think need to be improved?
What are the areas or issues you feel should be addressed?
The stories of leadership in this section show how one person
can make a difference through her leadership ability.
As you think about school leadership, remember that
a school leader doesn't have to be appointed or elected
to an office. A leader is someone who searches for
challenges and initiates positive change. A leader
organizes others toward a common goal.

Jennifer Kyer

LET'S USE IT AGAIN

JENNIFER KYER *is 11 years old and has always lived in New Jersey. Her family includes her mother, older brother, and her dog, as well as a few hamsters and mice. She is close to her cousins and grandmother, who live near her, and she misses her grandfather who died a few years ago.*

Jennifer's favorite hobbies include drawing and writing stories. She also loves to play soccer and ride horses.

When she was in the fourth and fifth grades, Jennifer won first place in the tri-community spelling bee. In 1992, she won a local newspaper contest titled "Pride in Your Neighborhood" for her recycling efforts at her school. Jennifer was also named a semifinalist in the national "Take Pride in America" competition. She and her mother traveled to Washington, D.C., to attend the national ceremony.

Recently, Jennifer was one of 15 students statewide to win an essay competition called "Passport to New Jersey," in which she visited two state attractions of historical or educational interest and wrote about them. In Trenton, the state capital, Lucinda Florio, the First Lady of New Jersey, met the students and presented them with prizes and certificates.

Jennifer's future goals include helping the Earth in any way she can and becoming an animal breeder for animals of all shapes and sizes.

$\mathcal{W}$HEN I WAS IN FOURTH GRADE, MY CLASS studied our state government and its officials. As part of our social studies class, each student pretended to be governor of New Jersey by learning about town, county, and state government. I wrote a letter to James Florio, the governor of New Jersey, and invited him to our class to see what we were studying. He said he would visit us.

During his talk to our class, the governor spoke about the importance of recycling. He said we should recycle as much as possible to save the environment. After his talk, I decided to get our school to recycle some of its trash.

Most of the students in my school bring their lunches every day and eat them in a lunchroom. We always have a lot of garbage at lunchtime. In the summer before I began fifth grade, I met with my school principal to work out a lunchtime recycling program and develop ideas to let all students know the importance of recycling.

In addition to meeting with the principal, I wrote to over 100 organizations and companies asking their advice about recycling. I received many items that explained recycling, such as posters, videos, curriculum guides, and stickers. I put the posters around the school and shared all the materials so students would be more aware of the need to recycle.

Jennifer Kyer collects trash for recycling

To get some town support for my program, I attended a mayor and council meeting at my Town Hall. I spoke about recycling and the lunchtime program we were developing at school.

For the recycling program, I decided to collect cans, paper products, and plastics. I placed three bins in the lunchroom and made signs asking students to separate their trash. My town agreed to send trucks to pick up the bins and take them to a local recycling center.

Many students took the time to separate their trash and the recycling program became a success. It's still in operation today.

Most of the people I wrote to and spoke with about recycling helped me with ideas. My principal encouraged me very much. I didn't meet many obstacles, except it was hard to find a time when my principal could meet with me to set up the program and approve my ideas.

When I was in sixth grade, I worked on a large can recycling drive. My school made arrangements with the county to pick up the cans we had collected. The county weighed the cans and paid my school money for each pound of cans we gave them. I would like to see as much trash as possible recycled at my school and in my town.

I believe my recycling projects helped many students learn about the importance of recycling. Also, the school has learned that a student can contribute good ideas to help everyone. Sometimes kids really come up with worthwhile things!

I plan to use my abilities to help save Mother Earth in any way I can. My advice to any student who wants to become a more effective leader is to choose a worthwhile idea or project and then motivate others to help you put your idea into action.

WHAT YOU CAN DO

▶ Is there a need for more environmental awareness in your school or community? To find out, conduct a survey of students or community members. After analyzing the information from your survey, develop and implement a plan for action.

▶ Competition for a good cause can be fun. Start a recycling competition between grades at your school or between schools in your community.

▶ Find out if your school or community has an active club focusing on environmental issues. If it does, consider becoming a member. If it doesn't, why not start one?

▶ Do senior citizens in your community know all the ways to recycle? If they don't, develop an interesting program to present to civic groups, churches, nursing homes, retirement communities, and other groups for seniors.

FIND OUT MORE, GET INVOLVED

Keep America Beautiful, Incorporated
Mill River Plaza
9 West Broad Street
Stamford, CT 06902

Provides information about ways you can get involved to beautify your community.

Kids Against Pollution
Tenakill School
275 High Street
Closter, NJ 07624

Sends out information on this networking group that works to stop pollution.

U.S. Environmental Protection Agency
Office of External Relations and Education
Youth Programs (A-108)
401 M Street, SW
Washington, DC 20460

Provides educational materials about the environment for students in kindergarten through twelfth grade.

Lawren Olenchak

THE PLIGHT
OF THE DOLPHINS

Many activities occupy 12-year-old LAWREN OLENCHAK'S
life. She likes school and has won awards through her involvement in school activities, including the science fair, spelling
bees, Quiz Bowl/ Knowledge Master, and art contests. She
enjoys drama and has acted in school and community plays.
For two years, she was president of her Girl Scout troop.
Currently, she is treasurer of her seventh grade class at
Tuscaloosa Academy in Tuscaloosa, Alabama. Some of
Lawren's hobbies include reading, French, choir, and other
school- and church-related projects. In addition to her other
activities, Lawren runs a three-year-old business that sells
symmetrically painted pajamas.

Lawren's mother works part-time as a neonatal intensive
care nurse at a local hospital. Her father is the area head of the
College of Education at the University of Alabama. When
Lawren grows up, she would like to go through law school and
someday become the first female president of the United States.

$\mathcal{M}$Y STORY BEGINS WHEN I WAS IN A FIFTH-grade enrichment class at Verner Elementary School in Tuscaloosa, Alabama. My class had been talking about recycling and about the killing of animals. One day, my teacher showed us a video about the slaughtering of dolphins. The video not only made me sad that these animals were being killed, but also made me angry that people could be so cruel to animals. In the video, I saw children my age who had helped save the animals. Most of them had drawn posters that made people aware of what was going on. When the video was over, I decided I wanted to help the dolphins, too.

The next day, I told my teacher that I wanted to find out why the dolphins were being killed. She gave me some articles and I collected books on the subject from the public library. After reading the articles, I learned that some tuna companies are responsible for many dolphin deaths each year. These companies use large nets to catch tuna. Dolphins are attracted to these nets because the dark net color is so different from their usual coral habitat. When the tuna fishermen haul in the nets, which are the right size for tuna but too small for dolphins, the dolphins become tangled. As a result, they choke and die. The fishermen throw the dead dolphins back into the water.

By the time I had researched the topic of tuna companies and dolphins, I had urged two of my friends to help me. I created a lesson about the plight of the dolphins that my two friends and I rehearsed. I told teachers that our group could teach the lesson to their classes. I made a sign announcing the lesson and pinned it to the bulletin board in the teachers' workroom. A few teachers signed up right away.

Our first presentation was to our own class. The students enjoyed it, and we convinced them that they could help solve the problem.

The next day, I was to present my lesson to a kindergarten class. I knew the younger students would not understand the lesson if I used the same procedure I had used with older students. I searched for another method. From the school library, I borrowed a puppet stage that our librarian used to teach younger children their letters and numbers. Using a puppet that resembled a whale, I put on a puppet show for the kindergarten class. My whale puppet told the story of the cruelty to the dolphins. The children loved it! I went on to present my lesson to almost every class in the school.

In my lesson, the main thing I told the students is that we need to do something about this problem, but that for any solution we will need money. I then described Greenpeace's dolphin adoption program I had read about. For a fee, anyone could adopt a dolphin from this environmental group.

I asked all of the students if they could bring in a penny, quarter, or any amount and put it in my "dolphin can" in the school office. I told them that with their help, I would try to collect enough money to save a dolphin. Many children said they thought they could bring in some money. Some even gave up their quarters for ice cream at lunch!

Four months later and three weeks before school was out for summer vacation, I counted the money. The principal let me announce over the school intercom that we had collected exactly $250. That was enough money to adopt two adult dolphins and one baby. I filled out the forms Greenpeace had sent me and mailed them with our money. On the last day before vacation, we received a letter announcing that Verner Elementary School was the proud "parent" of three dolphins.

Lawren Olenchak begins her lesson on the plight of the dolphins

Collecting money and adopting three dolphins may have been a small project, but I feel good because I taught others about the problems of the dolphins. Even though I am now in middle school, I am happy that my elementary school did something about this environmental cruelty. I hope to continue helping others as I move on through school. I like helping people and would be glad to participate in another project like this again.

If someone else chose to do a similar project, I would advise that person to get assistance from an adult and open a bank account that collects interest. One of my main concerns throughout this project was that someone would steal the money that was being collected in the school office. If I had put the money in a bank account, that would not have been a worry.

I would also advise everyone to follow their dreams. Many people told me that my ideas were ridiculous, but I ignored their statements. If you follow your dreams, who knows what may come about from them.

I will continue to follow my ideas because I know that if we abuse our environment to the point where there is nothing left, humans may be the endangered species in the future. I plan to do all I can to encourage others to do their part in protecting our world. I love to lead others so that they may become what they want to be.

WHAT YOU CAN DO

▶ Find out about other animals that need to be saved. Make a list and research those in which you are most interested. Design posters, pamphlets, or other materials to let people in your school and community know about an animal you want to save. How can you start a project in your school or community to save these animals?

▶ If Lawren had not been able to raise money in her school for the dolphins, how could she have raised money in the community?

▶ Investigate to find out if there are animal issues in your own community that need to be addressed, such as what to do with stray cats and dogs. Form a plan of action for solving these problems.

▶ Organize student volunteers to help at the local animal shelters. Initiate an adopt-a-pet program. Conduct a city-wide pet parade for unwanted pets to help them get adopted.

FIND OUT MORE, GET INVOLVED

American Oceans Campaign
725 Arizona Avenue, Suite 102
Santa Monica, CA 90401

Provides information on the preservation of the oceans' natural environment.

American Society for the Prevention of Cruelty to Animals (ASPCA)
Education Department
441 East 92nd Street
New York, NY 10128

Offers information on the humane treatment of animals.

Greenpeace
1436 U Street, NW
Washington, DC 20009

Provides information on a variety of environmental topics and programs.

World Wildlife Fund
1250 24th Street, NW
Washington, DC 20037

Offers information on the preservation of endangered species, rain forests, and wetlands.

Susan Jacobs

WRITING A BOOK TO PROMOTE UNDERSTANDING

Sixteen-year-old SUSAN JACOBS *lives in Charleston, West Virginia. She is the younger of two daughters, and her parents are divorced. Susan's mother has been remarried for six years, but her father remains single. Susan is close to her maternal grandparents, who live near her, and she spends as much time with them as possible. Susan has inherited many of her leadership abilities from her close-knit family.*

Susan's main interests are dancing, writing, and working in youth groups. She has taken dancing lessons since the age of four and hopes to continue for several more years. She often enters writing contests; the following story is an example of her writing ability. Susan is involved in local chapters of B'nai B'rith Youth Organization *and the National Conference of Synagogue Youth, two national youth groups. She is a chapter officer for both, and through both groups she finds opportunities to write, speak, organize events, and even dance.*

Susan has received many awards, including the Kanawha County Daughters of the American Revolution (DAR) essay award, third place in the Optimist Oratory in the Charleston finals, third place for Oratory in her junior high County Speech Contest, and third place in the county spelling bee, as well as citizenship awards. She also has been appointed to the National Junior Honor Society and Principals' Honor Roll and was named Student of the Month.

Susan is currently involved in a youth group that works with "Operation Awareness," a program run with people who have physical disabilities. She hopes to continue telling others about her leadership experiences.

Her career plans are still indefinite, but Susan has considered becoming a lawyer and definitely wants to incorporate writing into her career.

I BEGAN ASSISTING STUDENTS WITH physical disabilities when I was in sixth grade. (Sometimes, people with disabilities are called "handicapped," but it's not fair to call them that because the word places limits on their abilities.) My class had a partnership with some students at Edgewood Acres, a school for students with special physical needs. During that year, I found out that some of the students I was getting to know would be going to junior high with me in the fall.

A few days into my first year at Horace Mann Junior High School, I was able to get my schedule changed so that I could work with my friends from the year before. All through seventh and eighth grades, for one period a day, I was a student assistant in a room designated as a resource center for students with disabilities. We did all sorts of creative activities, basically anything that was a nontraditional classroom activity.

One day, I talked with my friends about how it felt to be in a wheelchair and to have a disability. As we talked, I was reminded of an episode from the television show "Life Goes On," in which a substitute teacher inspired a class of students with disabilities to create a play about their feelings. Somehow as we talked, the idea for a booklet materialized. We decided to create a booklet where the students could express their struggles and frustrations.

That day, another student assistant and I began to write down the feelings the students dictated to us. We interviewed the students to find out their likes and dislikes and other personal information. From this information, I wrote short biographies of the students to accompany their stories. The students each drew a picture that would be included in the booklet. Later, I wrote an introduction for the booklet and a short explanation of each student's disability. The other student assistant drew a cover for the booklet. We titled our booklet "What It Feels Like To Be Me."

After I typed all of the written work, the special education teacher photocopied the finished product so that each participant could have a copy. It was such a hit that the principal decided to make a copy for every student in the school. I had hoped that other students would have access to this creation, but I hadn't had the nerve to actually tell anyone this. Now my dream had come true.

Susan Jacobs, second from right, visits some of her friends with physical disabilities

A couple of days later, every student in the school received a copy of the booklet that had started out as a crazy fantasy for me; it felt wonderful. Many people were moved by this compilation of silent emotions. What I had written was merely a collection of the precious words of my courageous friends. I was just an assistant for their expression. I don't know what it feels like to be them, but I talked to them as equals. Making this booklet gave me a lot of insight into their emotions.

The students with disabilities, their teacher, and I had hoped that this booklet would change the way other students viewed students with disabilities. Although not everyone's feelings have changed, at least for a little while the students of my school were forced to see their peers in a new light.

A year before we created the booklet, the students with disabilities would sit by themselves in the hallways of Horace Mann Junior High, only occasionally talking to someone. Now, when these students are in the halls, they are often bombarded with friendly attention, and at the very least, usually get a "hello." I think my friends with disabilities still feel segregated by their physical abilities and probably always will, but at least there are more people who say hello to them, instead of just staring at them. I would like to think the booklet is responsible for this change, but I think the attitudes of students in the school and the great personalities of my friends with disabilities have had more to do with the changes.

I received recognition in a school assembly for my work on the booklet, but my greatest reward was seeing all of my classmates leafing through the booklet and perhaps stopping to think for a few moments.

I realize that my situation is somewhat unique; most students don't have the opportunity to set aside class time to work on leadership activities. However, all students can take advantage of opportunities to help their peers with disabilities. For students in schools that don't provide volunteer or leadership opportunities, I would advise them to become involved in a youth group or community center.

WHAT YOU CAN DO

▶   Are there students with disabilities in your school? If so, how do other students treat them? Think about how you could conduct a project similar to Susan's in your school or community. What could you do to make others more aware of these students and their special needs?

▶   Examine your school and community to determine how accessible they are to individuals with disabilities. Are there ramps or elevators available for people who cannot walk up stairs? Are drinking fountains low enough so that someone in a wheelchair can use them? If not, what can you do to help these areas become accessible to all people?

▶   Susan developed a booklet to inform others about individuals with physical disabilities. Think of other ways in which people could be informed about people with disabilities, or think of another topic you want people to know about. What would be the best way to present the information about your topic? Should you develop a flier, booklet, brochure, pamphlet, or poster? What research would be needed to prepare the informational piece?

FIND OUT MORE, GET INVOLVED

Foundation for Exceptional Children
1920 Association Drive
Reston, VA 22091

Has information about programs that focus on the needs of individuals with disabilities.

Muscular Dystrophy Association
810 Seventh Avenue
New York, NY 10019

Offers information about muscular dystrophy, a disease that causes a person's muscles to slowly weaken and become useless.

National Handicapped Sports
451 Hurgerford Drive, Suite 100
Rockville, MD 20850

Will send information on programs that make people aware of the needs and issues affecting people with physical disabilities.

National Multiple Sclerosis Society
205 East 42nd Street
New York, NY 10017

Offers information about multiple sclerosis, a disease that affects a person's central nervous system and causes speech defects and loss of muscle coordination.

National Wheelchair Athletic Association
3595 East Fountain Boulevard, Suite L-I
Colorado Springs, CO 80910

Provides materials on sporting activities for people with physical disabilities.

Mary Beth Brockmeier

A LESSON IN PERSISTENCE

Seventeen-year-old MARY BETH BROCKMEIER *has volunteered over 300 hours of her time to the United Way, local shelters, and nursing homes. She holds leadership positions in Amnesty International, the Michigan Junior Classical League, National Honor Society, Students Against Drunk Driving (SADD), and the student council. She also works part-time.*

Mary Beth *serves on advisory boards for the Voluntary Action Center in Holland, Michigan, the Holland Community Foundation, and the Michigan Youth Progressive Action Council, to which she was appointed by Governor John Engler.*

Mary Beth *has received numerous service awards, including membership in the Points of Light Foundation established by President George Bush. She participated in the National Junior Classical League convention, Junior Achievement International Student Forum, and Michigan's Summer Institute program.*

As a result of her assertiveness, she participated in two internships. For one, Mary Beth worked with the Greater Holland United Way to create a "Wish Book," which described the nonprofit organizations in her area. The other internship was with the Center for Women in Transition, which provides shelters for abused women and their children. Mary Beth helped to develop activities for the children in these shelters.

Mary Beth lives with her mother, who teaches Head Start classes; her father, who is a college professor; and an older brother, who attends college. She plans to attend a small private college and pursue the field of child development after graduating from Holland High School.

"*HELLO, I'M 16 YEARS OLD AND A JUNIOR* at Holland High School." Perhaps this was not the most interesting speech introduction the Holland Board of Education heard that night, but every board member shifted his or her eyes from their work to me.

My reason for addressing the board was to get the members to reconsider their proposal for increased co-curricular payments, which are the fees students pay to participate in extra-curricular activities. Just days before the meeting, the board members had listed in their agenda a proposal to raise the co-curricular payments from $15 an activity to $30.

My main objection to this fee increase involved Dutch Dancing, a tradition in our city's large annual Tulip Time Festival. During my sophomore year at Holland High School, I had become involved in this activity because I wanted to be a part of the festival.

The administration's proposal would require students to pay $30 for the privilege to dance, even though dancers already pay over

Mary Beth Brockmeier

$100 for the required wooden shoes, authentic costume, and transportation. Because Holland High School re-introduced Dutch Dancing to the community and because the festival depends on these dancers, I considered the fee increase ridiculous and unnecessary. In addition to Dutch Dancing, the board proposed fee increases for many other educational programs, including Close-Up and Model United Nations.

Before my presentation to the board, I researched the issue. I talked with the Dutch Dancing coordinator, board president, Holland High School principal, the Teacher's Union negotiator, teachers, co-curricular advisers, numerous peers, and newspaper reporters, to name a few.

By the time the board met, I had written a petition that asked the association to keep the rates as they were. Three hundred people signed my petition in the two days before the meeting.

After I introduced myself to the board, I submitted my petition. I pointed out how Dutch Dancers already pay for their costumes and that I felt a fee increase was not needed.

My first victory was only a partial one. The board members tabled my issue, which meant that they didn't want to make a decision now, but that they might deal with the issue later.

When the same fee proposal appeared on the agenda three months later, I rounded up friends and spoke again to the board members to remind them of the reasons for our prior petitioning. When, almost unanimously, the board voted the issue down, I knew that I had completed my goal.

I am proud to know that through my leadership, my fellow students will save hundreds of dollars. Because the board did not raise the fee, more students will be able to participate in the valuable traditions at Holland High School. I also feel that I have shown others that being a leader can be rewarding, especially when goals are met.

I will continue to use my leadership abilities at Holland High School and throughout the community because I have found that the road of leadership is both challenging and rewarding. Some of the ways I plan to continue this route are participating in events, volunteering, and youth and peer counseling through programs such as student council, United Way, and SADD (Students Against Drunk Driving).

How can others become better leaders? I have found that for me the key to advancement is assertiveness. It is also easier to complete a goal when you identify the needs of those involved and the actions required to meet a goal. Lastly, I feel that the most important step is to follow through with persistence. When I follow through, I feel successful because I have tried my best even if I never reached my goal.

Sometimes, the best leaders are those who have never quite gotten there. Although they may not be well known, these leaders are successful because they consistently strive for their goals. I have great admiration for them and hope that I can be as persistent.

WHAT YOU CAN DO

▶ Make a list of things that need to be changed, improved, or added to your school and community. Choose one or two issues. What are the best strategies for approaching them? Do you think petitions would help? If so, find out the appropriate procedure for petitioning. Do you need to design and present a proposal to the school board or city council? Remember to back up your proposal with good research.

▶ Mary Beth learned that persistence can pay off. She kept up with what the school board was doing and made sure the members didn't forget her petition. Think about a time in your life when your persistence has been beneficial. Was there a time or situation in your life in which you wish you had been more persistent? Is persistence a characteristic of leadership?

▶ Mary Beth said that "for me the key to advancement is assertiveness. What is the difference between assertiveness, passivity, and aggressiveness?

FIND OUT MORE, GET INVOLVED

The Children's Defense Fund
122 C Street, NW
Washington, DC 20001

This organization provides a voice for the children of the United States. Write to the Children's Defense Fund for information about protecting your rights.

International League for Human Rights
432 Park Avenue South, Suite 1103
New York, NY 10016

Will send information on how this organization fights for the promotion and protection of human rights across the globe.

Lawyers Committee for Human Rights
330 Seventh Avenue, 10th Floor North
New York, NY 1001

Shares information on how this advocacy group promotes human rights for everyone.

Francine Gold

ORGANIZING A CO-ED Y CLUB

FRANCINE GOLD, 15, *is a freshman at Henderson South Junior High School in Henderson, Kentucky. She is the daughter of Steven D. and Elaine Gold. Recently, Francine served as governor of the Kentucky Youth Assembly and presided over 1,300 delegates. The conference, sponsored by the state YMCA, was the largest mock legislature in the nation. During the conference, Francine was the recipient of the Kenton Memorial Award, which is awarded yearly to one delegate who displays outstanding leadership qualities. Her name has been engraved on a plaque that is permanently housed in the Capitol Building in Frankfort, Kentucky.*

Francine is treasurer of the student council and president and founder of the Co-Ed Y. She has also served as parliamentarian of the Beta Club. In addition to her activities, she has maintained an "A" average and participated in school sports, including varsity tennis. For relaxation, Francine plays the piano and drums. Her personal motto is, "Always go for the Gold."

$\mathcal{W}$HEN I FIRST THOUGHT ABOUT
organizing a Co-Ed Y club at our school, I didn't think it would be so
hard. Many other junior highs in Kentucky had such clubs, so why
shouldn't we, I had asked myself.

The Co-Ed Y club is a Christian-based organization. It is
affiliated with the state YMCA (Young Men's Christian Association),
which is school and community service oriented. I felt that my junior
high school could easily qualify for a club. Our students already
participated in the state YMCA-sponsored Kentucky Youth Assembly
and Kentucky United Nations Assembly. We had plenty to offer:
dedication, talent, and a nucleus of students familiar with the Y
club's principles and activities. Some of us had already thought
about school and community needs we could address once we
became a club. With these advantages, starting a club looked easy.
Was I ever mistaken!

I spent most of my eighth-grade year working on the formation
of this club. I first had to obtain approval for the club from school
authorities at my junior high. They were supportive but said I
needed to find a sponsor prior to approval.

In December of my eighth-grade year, I campaigned for election
as governor of the Kentucky Youth Assembly. The three-day campaign seemed simple in comparison to my lengthy effort to find a
sponsor for our Y club. My campaign was a success; I was voted
governor of the assembly.

On the day of the election, I started planning the statewide
conference for the following year, but the needs of the community
and school were still on my mind. On the way home from the conference, I heard a song by the Four Tops called "Ain't Too Proud to
Beg." The song inspired me to plan my course of action. I would go
to every classroom and beg for a sponsor. Most of the teachers were
overwhelmed with work, extra-curricular activities, or personal
commitments. They didn't want to take on more responsibilities. No
one wanted to become our sponsor. A few months later, I made the
same rounds and met with the same disappointing results. Toward
the end of the year, I added a commercial to the announcements
that were televised in each classroom and actually found a sponsor!

Our new sponsor had been in a Y club at her high school and felt that we should also be given this great opportunity.

The next step was to promote the club. Through personal contacts, I gathered a small group of students who were interested in the Y club. I made posters, announcements, and videotaped commercials, which were shown on the school television sets, to make sure everyone understood the purpose of the club. I also wanted them to know what a great club it would be. My friends and I spoke to each junior high class to create interest and enthusiasm. I also arranged for a representative of the state YMCA to present a program to prospective members. We soon had over 25 students anxious to start the club.

Elections were held to select officers for the club's initial year of activities. I was delighted and honored to be elected president because of all the hard work and time that I had put into organizing the club.

The officers and I met during the summer between eighth and ninth grades. We organized the club and planned the activities for the inaugural year. We began by planning one community and one school project each month, a Y club requirement. Before the school year started, we had performed our first school project. We assisted the teachers in the preparation of their classrooms and gave tours of the school to new students.

Francine Gold, center, works at a phone-a-thon to benefit a student injured in an accident

We began the school year with a membership drive. The highlight of this campaign was a skit performed before the student body that I wrote and coordinated. The skit was a takeoff on the song "Rawhide," which we called "Y Drive." As a result of these efforts, we formally installed 74 charter members in the Henderson South Junior High School Co-Ed Y Club. Thus, our club commenced its existence as the largest service-oriented club in our school.

Our community involvement began early with the occurrence of a local tragedy. A sophomore at our county high school was paralyzed following a truck accident. The Co-Ed Y members worked each evening for a week in a phone-a-thon to raise money to help pay for medical costs.

Also during the first two months, we helped the Knights of Columbus raise money for people with mental disabilities and provided a fund for the Hurricane Andrew victims. Club members helped with our school's tutorial program by volunteering their time and knowledge to help students who were having trouble understanding certain subjects. We also had a Pet Parade for our local Humane Society. We took the animals from the shelter and paraded them in our Central Park. Many people found it in their hearts to give homes to these animals.

As a result of our activities during the first two months of the school year, our club qualified for statewide recognition and awards based upon annual accomplishments.

We planned some other great projects, including visits to nursing homes and animal shelters and excursions to government office buildings to see our government in action. We also planned to create videos about the governmental process and the United Nations for teachers to use.

Two books, which I keep in my briefcase, have influenced me as a leader. Both are based on female role models. They are *The Little Engine That Could* and *The Little Red Hen*. I used the persistence and positive attitude displayed by both characters in the formation of the Co-Ed Y club. Just like the train who needed assistance from the engine, I, too, needed assistance from a sponsor. Both the train and

I met with rejection many times, but we did not give up and we reached our goal.

In my role as a state and local leader, I have found much merit in the story of *The Little Red Hen*. The Little Red Hen is anxious to include others in her project; that is the preferred method to accomplish a goal. In any leadership role, one encounters people who are unwilling to assist in any project but who are anxious to have the program implemented. Worse than the scenario of the Little Red Hen are those who say they will do a job but do not deliver. In either case, the leader must be prepared to "do it herself." Just as the Little Red Hen demonstrated that only a participant may reap the bounty, a leader must *never* give credit where credit is not due. On the other hand, a leader must *absolutely* make sure that deserving workers receive their just reward.

Sometimes a leader has to know when to show authority. Ideally, all officers in a club should cooperate, delegate responsibility, and share in the limelight. On occasion, one officer may try to usurp the authority that the other officers, including the president, may have. This is called a power play. The most effective and least damaging way to confront this problem is what I call the Barney Fife method, named after a character on "The Andy Griffith Show." Whenever Barney was faced with a problem, he'd say, "Nip it in the bud." Go directly to the source and firmly clarify the matter, leaving no doubt that the undermining efforts will be unsuccessful.

No matter what office you may hold or what responsibilities you may have, it is absolutely essential that you remember your purpose and seek advice whenever needed and from any source that may be helpful. Most important, have fun and enjoy what you are doing. If you have fun and a positive attitude about your organization, so will the other members. Your organization will be what you make it: boring and uneventful or fun, exciting and productive.

WHAT YOU CAN DO

▶ Does your school or community need a new club? If it does, develop a way to get it started. Think about the purpose of the club and set its goals. What obstacles do you expect to encounter as you plan your new club? How will you overcome these obstacles? How will you motivate others to join the club?

▶ Francine was inspired by a song, "Ain't Too Proud to Beg," and two books, *The Little Engine That Could* and *The Little Red Hen*. What are the songs or books that inspire you? Are there other things that inspire you?

▶ Francine warns about power plays that leaders often experience. How would you handle this kind of problem?

FIND OUT MORE, GET INVOLVED

Boys and Girls Club of America
771 First Avenue
New York, NY 10017

Offers awards for young people who have contributed to home, school, church, community, and Boys and Girls clubs. Write to them for more information.

Camp Fire, Incorporated
4601 Madison Avenue
Kansas City, MO 64112-1278

This organization encourages self-reliance and good citizenship and will send information on its activities.

4-H
7100 Connecticut Avenue
Chevy Chase, MD 20815

4-H provides opportunities and resources in youth development. Write to this group for information on 4-H clubs in your area.

Girls Incorporated
30 East 33rd Street
New York, NY 10016

Will send information about programs and services for girls ages 6 to 18. These programs include encouragement in math and science, drug and alcohol prevention, and teen pregnancy prevention.

YMCA of the USA
101 North Wacker Drive
Chicago, IL 60606

Sends information on how to increase your self-esteem and eliminate racism. For information on starting a Co-Ed Y club at your school, contact your local YMCA office.

Kate Budd

THE S.A.V.E. PROGRAM OF BALDWIN HIGH

Ahead of every young person lie opportunities to learn, grow, experience, and love. These chances diminish, however, as our planet is increasingly threatened. As 17-year-old KATE BUDD began to realize the state of our world, she saw that the aspirations of her peers would be impaired if no one acted to save the Earth first. Motivated by this knowledge and supported by her family, Kate cooperatively founded Students Aware of the Value of Earth (S.A.V.E.) at Baldwin High School in Pittsburgh, Pennsylvania.

Since 1991, the group has recycled thousands of pounds of newspapers and held an Earth Day Fair attended by more than 1,500 students. S.A.V.E. received recognition from members of the Pittsburgh community and was featured in local papers and on radio. For her work with S.A.V.E., Kate received the prestigious Rachel Carson Award from Chatham College. This annual award is given to a high school student who has contributed to the field of science, in particular environmental studies.

As she studies and works in the field of communications, Kate continues to let people know of her environmental concerns. In this way, she hopes to open the eyes of the public so that together we can make a lasting difference.

$\mathcal{D}$UE TO POLLUTION, MANY OF THE LAKES found in industrial countries are biologically dead. Plant and animal species become extinct daily. Does anyone know the long-term effects? Who or what will be affected next? The sky, water, and rain are polluted with pesticides and toxins.

The condition of the environment has always concerned me. This is the environment in which we live and which we intend to leave to future generations. Fear is widespread, indifference isn't uncommon; but, for many, the question of "What to do?" arises.

I tried to do what I could to help the Earth. I recycled and conserved energy. I knew my share helped, but I also knew that I could accomplish more if others helped me. Stephania Yee, a friend of mine, had the same idea.

When we were juniors at Baldwin High School, we both felt that working with a group would be stronger in quantity, and, hopefully, in quality than working individually. A group dedicated to recycling could really make an impact by attracting more attention and attempting larger tasks. Together, we decided to start an environmental organization at our school. We already had come up with a name: Students Aware of the Value of Earth, or S.A.V.E.

We knew that organizing a group would be a large job, but our enthusiasm was strong. Our first task was to get through the mechanics of starting a school club. We had to find a staff member who would be willing to sponsor us. My social studies teacher seemed like the obvious choice because he is a contemporary, open-minded teacher who is always enthusiastic about causes. He listened to our idea and agreed to sponsor us. Next, we filled out permission forms so that we could use school facilities for our meetings, which would be held twice a month after school for about an hour. Permission was granted.

Before we planned our first meeting, however, we thought about S.A.V.E.'s goals. What did we want to work toward? We had to keep our goals realistic and achievable; a lot would depend on the dedication, motivation, and number of group members. We also had to consider what our school would allow us to do. The members we hoped to attract would be new at working in a club—as we were. And, since we were the first organization of this kind at our school, we had no prior records to help us. To get some ideas, we wrote to several schools about their clubs. Their ideas helped, but we had to plan goals for our unique club. After hours of discussion, we came up with what we thought were several workable goals. Education was to be our group's first priority. The club had to be knowledge-able about the environment and the realities of the problem. Based on this knowledge, we eventually hoped to make the entire student body and our community more aware of the environmental crisis. We wanted to make a positive difference in our school and community to help the Earth.

The future of our group depended on the outcome of the first meeting, because what we could accomplish would depend on the impression we received from the students at that meeting. With that fact in mind, we planned down to the minute and advertised for the first meeting throughout the school. Our biggest fear was that few people would show up. But we told ourselves that even if we only had a few members, we would work hard and gain respect so that more people would get involved. With this philosophy, we walked into the first meeting. We were excited and surprised to find about 25 people in the room. Not only were we surprised at the number of people, but we were excited to find that they had ideas, wanted to work, and were excited, too. S.A.V.E. officially began!

Since we had decided to stress education about the environ-ment, our first project was to create posters to put up around the school. We hoped to expose students and teachers to some of the situations in the environment. We invited people from local organi-zations such as Clean Water Action and the Group for Recycling in

Kate Budd works for S.A.V.E.

Pennsylvania to speak at our meetings. From these speakers, we gained knowledge about the local and national issues of recycling and toxic waste. Thanks to the speakers' information, we came up with project ideas, including writing letters to local and national officials and planting a garden. We elected publicity and treasury committees and organized our first recycling drive. We continued our education campaign by establishing an informational bulletin board in the hall at school.

At times, our progress seemed slow, but S.A.V.E.'s members remained dedicated; we knew that everything we did counted. It is very motivating when members ask about an upcoming event or ask if there is anything they can do. It's great when someone has an idea or makes a poster without being asked. We knew that our club was succeeding because people were thinking about the environment— and doing something about it!

Our next major projects were for the spring, when we started a garden and organized an Earth Day Fair, which included a week of environmental awareness involving everyone in the school. We continued our work as seniors while we provided for our successors and prepared them to continue our work.

Personally, my goals for this project have been to make a positive difference in terms of the environment and to establish an organization that will continue long after I graduate. Because the challenge of setting up S.A.V.E. did not intimidate us, we have given other students a chance to join a club and help a worthwhile cause.

The best advice I can give to young adults is not to be afraid of leadership and to just get involved. If you think you can't do it, think about what could be—think about the difference you could make and see if this doesn't outweigh the sacrifices. Remember that success comes with time. Nothing truly worthwhile comes instantly. Each of us can do so much; together we can do more.

WHAT YOU CAN DO

▶ Does your school need a club that focuses on environmental issues? Think about how you could organize one in your school. Kate said she knew her club was successful when members got involved and acted on their own to come up with ideas and posters. How would you know if your club was successful?

▶ Brainstorm a list of ways your school or community can help to save the Earth. Design a poster to let other students know about your concern for the environment.

▶ Think about the types of clubs or organizations that need to be developed in your school and community. How could you get such groups organized? What is the key ingredient for getting people started on such a project?

▶ Think about what you would do if you were elected or appointed to be the next leader of S.A.V.E. How would you motivate students to continue the club's work?

FIND OUT MORE, GET INVOLVED

Adopt a Stream Foundation
P.O. Box 5558
Everett, WA 98201

Offers guidelines for adopting a stream or wetland.

The Cousteau Society
930 West 21st Street
Norfolk, VA 23517

Write to this organization to receive materials on the environment and how to protect it.

The Student Conservation Association, Incorporated
P.O. Box 550
Charlestown, NH 03603

Provides opportunities for volunteer work in national parks and forests for students 16 years of age and older.

Washington State Department of Ecology Litter Control and Recycling Program
4350 150th Avenue, NE
Redmond, WA 98052

Sends materials on the environment for students in kindergarten through twelfth grade.

Cari Skogberg

TEACHING SIGN LANGUAGE
TO LEARN ABOUT OTHERS

CARI SKOGBERG, 19, *grew up in Belle Fourche, South Dakota, with her parents, John and Genevieve Skogberg, and her brother Cody. Although she has many interests, one of her favorites is learning about other cultures and countries. To pursue that interest, Cari corresponds with over 100 friends and pen pals from around the world and has traveled to Europe and Israel.*

As a result of her work teaching sign language to people, Cari was chosen as one of 50 honorable mention recipients in the Noxema Extraordinary Teen Contest. She was also the first high school sophomore recognized on the USA Today All USA High School Academic Team. *For three years, she earned a spot on the honorable mention team. Her writing, including an article on South Dakota and one on democracy, has been published in such documents as the* Congressional Record.

In 1992, when she graduated from Belle Fourche High School, Cari had enough credits to earn the equivalent of two diplomas. In the fall of 1992, she became a student at Augustana College in Sioux Falls, South Dakota, where she is pursuing degrees in education and foreign relations. She hopes to teach gifted children someday.

STOP FOR A MOMENT AND IMAGINE THAT you live in a world of complete silence. It's kind of eerie, isn't it? Thousands of deaf people live in this world of silence. Many hearing people think of the hearing impaired as mentally unequal or incapable. This misconception made me determined to teach people differently.

My interest in sign language was sparked at a young age. My aunt had a cousin who was deaf, and when I visited her she would teach me simple signs. Through the years, I practiced. During my sophomore year in high school, I read about a sign language course that would be offered at a nearby college. I knew that I was technically too young to take the course, but I was determined to learn to sign, so I obtained special permission from my principal and the sign language instructor and enrolled in the class. I am so glad that they had faith in my ability, because taking that course was one of the best things I have ever done! In fact, I enjoyed the class so much that when an advanced sign language course was offered the following spring, I jumped at the opportunity to enroll.

Through these courses, I learned American Sign Language (ASL). ASL is recognized as a true language that has its own system of grammar. Each sign in ASL consists of three parts: hand shape, location, and movement. Through ASL, deaf people can communicate abstract as well as concrete ideas. ASL advocates say that it is the most natural and efficient way for deaf individuals to learn about the world.

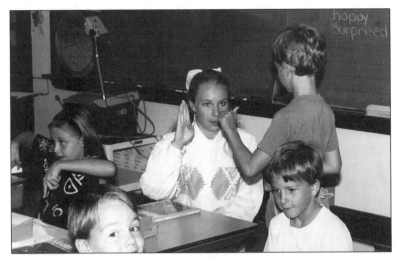

Cari Skogberg teaches signing at an elementary school

The best part about these courses was that our instructor not only taught us sign language, but she also taught us about the deaf culture and what it would be like to live as a deaf person in a hearing world. I had never thought about how isolated deaf people must sometimes feel. It is very difficult for them to learn the spoken language, but almost all hearing people have the ability to learn to sign. Few hearing people have made the effort to learn to sign, however. Some situations have ended tragically because a hearing person could not communicate with a deaf person.

During my junior year of high school, after I had completed both college courses, I demonstrated sign language to 4-H clubs, church groups, the school board, and anyone else who was interested. It was rewarding to see the smiles on peoples' faces as they learned to sign words or the alphabet. I especially loved teaching sign language to children, because of their limitless enthusiasm and interest. I asked my high school guidance counselor for permission to teach sign language as an independent study course to classes at a nearby elementary school. At first my request was met with a bit of apprehension because no one had ever done anything like this before. However, once I had completed a course outline and found a teacher supervisor to oversee my work, it was agreed that I could begin teaching. I was thrilled!

For the following three months, I spent 30 to 35 minutes a day with four fifth-grade classes and one fourth-grade class. I taught the students to sign the alphabet, words, and phrases, and told them a bit about the deaf culture. I knew that the kids would pick up this new language quickly, but I could hardly believe how quickly they learned! They loved it and practiced many hours both in and out of the classroom. I was so proud of them! When I saw my students in the grocery store or uptown, they would stop me and show me what they had been practicing. It was a wonderful feeling to know that they shared my enthusiasm for this language. Many parents even told me that their kids were teaching them how to sign.

By the end of the trimester, each classroom made a videotape of stories and songs in sign language, which I later sent to the children at the South Dakota School for the Deaf. The videotape was a wonderful project that helped my students to understand how useful sign language could be.

My classes in the elementary school were such a success that I decided to share what I had learned with another generation in my town. At the local nursing home, I formed a new group of senior students called the "Sensational Signers." I taught the residents many of the same things that I had taught my younger students, as well as patriotic phrases and songs. They, too, loved learning how to sign. It gave them a wonderful sense of pride and accomplishment. Signing was also great therapy for the residents who had arthritis. One woman told me that after learning some sign language, she could finally communicate with her deaf grandson. Hearing stories like this made my work worthwhile. It was such a special feeling to know that my time and efforts had made a big difference in others' lives.

I continued to teach sign language during my senior year of high school. When I began college, I organized another sign language workshop at an elementary school.

My students have taught me just as much, or maybe more, than I have taught them. I have gained some wonderful teaching experience and have learned important skills which will benefit me throughout my life. I think that the most rewarding part of all is knowing that hundreds of kids look up to me and want to do the things that I do when they get older. *That* is what it's all about. It was great that I was able to teach them sign language, but it was even more wonderful to have sparked their interest in going above and beyond average activities and reaching for dreams that may have seemed out of reach before. I truly believe that *no* goal is impossible to reach, and *no* dream is too big. It may take hard work and determination, but anything can be accomplished if the will to accomplish it exists!

To me, being a leader means being a person who can make a difference in someone else's life. That may be accomplished in millions of different ways, through a kind word or a helping hand, or by setting an example for others to follow. To become a leader, you don't have to take college courses or pass a specific test. You only have to have the true desire to reach out to others and be a positive part of their lives.

The best advice that I could give to emerging leaders is to love who you are, have faith in yourself and your goals, and stand strong for what you believe in. There is no one else in the world like you— that alone makes you a special person! You have been blessed with wonderful gifts to share, so share them! *You* have the ability to make a positive impact on the world, so do it! You really *can* make a difference. I thank God each day for the gifts that He has given me. I pray that I will never waste them, but instead use them to the best of my ability. I hope the world will be a better place because I did!

WHAT YOU CAN DO

▶ Find out if classes for sign language are available in your school or community. If they are available, consider enrolling in a class. If there are no classes, find a book about sign language at your library. Perhaps you could teach yourself how to sign.

▶ As Cari learned sign language, she also learned about the deaf culture. How can you learn more about this group of people? How can you help others to learn about deaf people? Design an activity that lets hearing individuals experience a simulation of the world of deaf individuals.

▶ Find out the groups in your school and community that deaf or disabled children belong to and attend a meeting. Think about joining their group and helping out.

▶ Cari's definition of a leader is someone who can make a difference in another person's life. Think about how you would define leadership. How is your definition alike or different from Cari's definition?

FIND OUT MORE, GET INVOLVED

Alexander Graham Bell Association for the Deaf
3417 Volta Place, NW
Washington, DC 20007
Encourages the communication of hearing-impaired individuals and offers information on hearing impairment.

American Society for Deaf Children
814 Thayer Avenue
Silver Springs, MD 20910
Promotes positive attitudes towards signing and the deaf culture and provides current information about deafness.

Self Help for Hard of Hearing People
7800 Wisconsin Avenue
Bethesda, MD 20814
Provides information to educate the general public on deafness and hearing impairment.

Alexis Hunter

THOUGHTS LEAD TO ACTION

ALEXIS HUNTER *is 18 years old and attends Brown University in Providence, Rhode Island. She is the daughter of G. William and Janice Hunter and the youngest of three children. Alexis was born and raised in Oakland, California, and attended Berkeley High School in Berkeley, California.*

During her four years at Berkeley High, Alexis played basketball and tennis. In her senior year, Alexis was co-captain of her basketball team and, despite a knee injury that sidelined her from competition during the pre-season, led her team to the semifinals of the state championship. In tennis, Alexis received a northern California state ranking and played in the number two position for the high school's tennis team. She won numerous trophies and helped Berkeley capture two league doubles titles for two consecutive years.

Alexis was co-vice president of her junior class, a peer tutor and counselor, a member of Jack and Jill of America, and continues to be an active member in the McGee Avenue Baptist Church in Berkeley.

Alexis loves to travel and has visited Australia, Honolulu, Maui, Fiji, Jamaica, Martinique, Mexico, and the Bahamas. During her junior year in college, she plans to study abroad for a semester. Although Alexis is undecided about her major, she is interested in environmental studies and public policy.

THE 1991–1992 SCHOOL YEAR WAS SUPPOSED to be the best of my high school career, and up until April 1992, two months before graduation, everything was going well. I had completed the college application process and had been admitted to Brown University, my first choice. I had completed my basketball career on a winning note and maintained a 4.0 grade point average. Most importantly, I was enjoying my last few weeks of school.

On April 29, 1992, my life changed. On that day, the nation heard the verdict on the first Rodney King trial. That day brought to the forefront racial and social issues I had pushed to the back of my mind during my senior year.

I first heard about Rodney King with the rest of the nation in 1991. In March of that year, in the wee hours of the night, a person operating a video camera recorded a violent scene that involved Rodney King, an African American, and four white police officers. The videotape, which appeared to show the police officers beating King, was shown on newscasts around the country.

When I first saw the videotape, I had a feeling that the police officers would never be convicted of the crime. Deep down, however, I hoped that the evidence shown in the videotape would be enough to convict the officers. The videotape and King's allegations led to a trial where the police officers argued that they were only subduing a prisoner. After reviewing the evidence, the jury decided that the police officers were not guilty.

After school on that April day, I went home, prepared a snack, and turned on the television as usual. But instead of the usual talk shows, the news of the jury's verdict dominated the screen. On every channel the verdict and reactions to the trial appeared. In Los

Angeles, about 350 miles south of Oakland, violence had broken out. In response to the not-guilty verdict, people were looting stores, rioting, and shooting others. For the next few hours, I sat and watched the news reports.

Despite my initial feeling about this case, when I heard the verdict I was overcome with anger. I was upset with the world and the justice system of this country. I felt as though I had no safe place to run, and I feared for my future and the future of my people. However, the more I watched the news, the more I realized that this situation would cause tension among the races at my high school the next day. I knew that if anything positive was to result from the Rodney King incident, it would take the efforts of every race to bring about change.

That night I got little sleep. My mind was on what I could do to make a difference. I wondered about the impact the verdict would have on the other 2,497 students at Berkeley High School, a school familiar with racial issues.

On my way to math class the following day, I realized that something about the school was different. The halls, which were usually filled with students and noise before classes, were deserted; before I walked into class I didn't know what to expect. No one was in the mood to discuss math and the expression on all faces was bleak. One of the five vice-principals gave my math teacher a note and he immediately read it out loud. The note said that the class period was to be spent discussing our feelings about the outcome of the trial and that during the next period students would march to the police station to let others know our opinions. I joined the discussion and told others about the impact the verdict had on my life and why I believed people looted and destroyed stores, neighborhoods, and buildings. For the most part, however, my attention was focused on getting involved in the march.

When the bell rang, I headed to the place where the march was to begin and stood near my friend who was in charge of the protest. As the march began, more and more students got involved; slowly the group began to cross in front of traffic. I began organizing everyone, making sure that people remained in the driving lanes opposite oncoming traffic, and leading the march to the police station, three blocks from our high school. Initially, the marchers were disjointed and it seemed as though many of the students were more concerned about leaving campus than accomplishing the objectives of the march. I grabbed a portable microphone out of my friend's hands and reminded the hundreds of students that we were going to the police station in peace to voice our opinions.

When we arrived at the Berkeley police station, my friend and I, along with a few others who had led the protest, situated ourselves on the steps of the station while everyone else filled the street and sidewalks surrounding the area. By this time others had gotten involved, including pedestrians, residents, newscasters, radio broadcasters, local elementary school students, and Berkeley High School faculty.

I got on the microphone and voiced my opinions on the Rodney King issue. I told the crowd what I felt our group could do to bring about change. I told everyone that education was the key; that even though there was little we as students could do now, we could focus our energy to make changes in the future. Through education we could put ourselves in positions of power, positions where we would have the authority to change things for the better. I also stressed the issue of every race working together toward change. If anything was to be accomplished, the effort would have to be made by everyone. We could no longer afford to segregate ourselves.

Alexis Hunter, center (with microphone), leads a peaceful march following the first Rodney King verdict

The crowd in front of the police station was excited by what I had to say. But I felt that this was not supposed to be an opportunity for me alone to vent some of my frustrations. It was an opportunity for everyone to vent their frustrations in a productive, positive way. Students, residents, administrators, and police officers of all nationalities voiced their opinions to the crowds. There were a few occasions when black students attacked white students and blamed them for the problems, but I quickly got on the microphone and told everyone that we could no longer afford to blame each other.

The media and police officers expected our group to react violently, like the crowds in Los Angeles, but that was not our objective. Our motives for marching were to inform the public that we did not agree with the Rodney King verdict and that our voices would be heard.

The uncertain feelings I had felt before coming to school were nonexistent after the peaceful march to the police station. Among all the chaos that arose from the Rodney King verdict, I felt that something positive had been accomplished and that change was feasible. After the march, everyone went their separate ways and most joined other marches, but I returned to class feeling optimistic about the future.

The school principal, my classmates, teachers, and local residents thanked me for taking charge of the protest and encouraging the crowd. By the end of the week, I had appeared in the school newspaper and on National Public Radio, had given a speech, and had received letters from people all over the country.

Until the march to the police station began, I had no idea that I would help to lead it. All I knew was that something had to be done and that leading and organizing the protest was one way to help. My advice to others is to take initiative and risks. The only prerequisites to leadership are that you remain positive, calm, and open-minded.

WHAT YOU CAN DO

▶ Much of today's society is plagued with racial tension. Examine specific behaviors and situations that have created racial tension in your school or community. In what ways can you prevent racial tension? How might you work to counteract racial stereotypes and misconceptions?

▶ Conduct interviews with people of all races and ages in your school and community and ask them about ways to improve race relations. Compile these ideas and choose some to put into action. Write articles for your school and community newspapers to highlight any improvements made in race relations. Some newspapers already report on the negative—make it your goal to put a positive emphasis on issues.

▶ Help younger children in your school and community understand people of other races. Plan a fun event, such as a puppet show, game, play, or book reading, to show younger children how different races can get along.

FIND OUT MORE, GET INVOLVED

Commission for Racial Justice
700 Prospect Avenue, 7th Floor
Cleveland, OH 44115

Offers programs and services for racial justice and social equality.

Congress of Racial Equality (CORE)
30 Cooper Square
New York, NY 10003

Sends out information on how to promote equality for all people.

National Association for the Advancement of Colored People (NAACP)
4805 Mt. Hope Drive
Baltimore, MD 21215-9297

The NAACP has information on how to work for equal rights and eliminate racial prejudice.

National Institute against Prejudice and Violence
31 South Greene Street
Baltimore, MD 21201

This research and public policy organization studies violence that is motivated by prejudice. Will send information about their findings.

People for the American Way
2000 M Street, NW, Suite 400
Washington, DC 20036

Provides information on civil liberties, constitutional rights, and public interest groups.

Cynthia Tanguilig

RECYCLING TO SAVE OUR PLANET

*A family of ten is so large you might be surprised to learn
that its members can be close to each other. Seventeen-year-
old CYNTHIA TANGUILIG from Charleston, West Virginia,
was nurtured not only by her parents, but also by her seven
brothers and sisters. As a result, her interests are varied.
Cynthia is her own unique individual. No one word can be
used to describe her—she doesn't want to fall into a pre-
dictable routine. She plans to do many things and experience
all of what life has to offer.*

    *Cynthia is satisfied and proud of her accomplishments
and recognitions. She is especially proud of being awarded
George Washington High School's Patriot Award, given to
the student who most represents the school's ideals. She also
strives for success in sports; in high school she was captain of
the varsity track and basketball teams. Her accomplishments,*

*along with her leadership on the student council, earned her
a scholarship to Ohio University in Athens. As a college
student, Cynthia has no regrets from high school—just fond,
precious memories and a statement that she stands by:
"Just do it."*

IN THE SUMMER BEFORE MY JUNIOR YEAR
in high school, I was reminded every day of the continuing plight of
our environment. I realized that people were throwing away many
items that could have been recycled. I was disgusted, to say the
least. With my friends, I discussed starting a recycling club at my
high school. Forming and maintaining the club would be difficult,
but it was something I felt was very necessary.

When I began my junior year at George Washington High
School, I received permission from our principal to start my
recycling project. I decided to start small and just recycle soda and
juice cans. As a member of the student council, I obtained the support of all the members. However, I knew I would need more help, so
I turned for support to the Key Club, another strong school group.
With members from both groups, I formed the Recycling Club.

Devising a system to store the cans was my first step. Metro
Recycling, a local recycling center, donated eight large cylindrical
bins. The Key Club members told me that their club, in cooperation
with a local construction company, planned to build a large recycling bin next to the trash bins on school property. The enthusiasm
continued to build.

At the next student council meeting, I informed the group of the
Recycling Club's progress. I also told them that the donated bins
had to be painted so that students could discern them from normal
trash bins. I suggested painting the bins to resemble large soda
cans; using the same colors as popular brands, but changing the
names to the school name or mascot. Although everyone was
receptive to this idea, no one on the student council or Key Club
offered to help.

After two weeks of no progress, I decided to paint the bins with the help of a single friend. Two bins had been damaged, which increased my desire to make the Recycling Club a success and encouraged me to work harder. We used donations from parents to buy paints and spent many hours working on the six cans. Although I am not an artist, I penciled in four different designs on our bins. With occasional help from friends, we finished painting the cans in six days. With the rest of the donations, I bought boxes of fifty-gallon trash bags that fit our new recycling receptacles. On a rainy night in late November, three of my friends and I put the recycling receptacles in strategic places throughout the school; the Recycling Club was off to a start.

Once the recycling bins were in place, interest in the club grew. By the end of the school year, the Recycling Club was the largest, smoothest running student organization in the school. It was a success! Twelve groups alternating on a weekly basis emptied the receptacles and brought the bags to the large recycling bin.

Cynthia Tanguilig with two of her hand-painted recycling bins

By the beginning of my senior year, I had doubled the number of recycling cans in the school and expanded the club to include computer paper. Although a few cans are still thrown in trash bins, many people recycle. I feel that if even thirty people make recycling a lifelong habit, their newfound awareness of the environment will be enough to touch the lives of others. I hope in college I can continue to encourage others to make our world a little nicer, a little cleaner. This is my planet, and I love it. I strongly feel that my generation must protect our Earth if we want a place for our children to live. We must make a difference.

To me, a good leader is one who guides others and lets them work for themselves so they feel a stronger sense of accomplishment. I know life isn't easy and that it's easy to be carried along. But only you can make your life as fulfilling as possible.

Anyone with determination and commitment can be a leader. Believing in yourself is all you need to do to accomplish anything— you just have to realize that. We can and must do something because, as John F. Kennedy said, "It's time for a new generation of leadership. . .for there is a new world to be won."

WHAT YOU CAN DO

▶ Outline a detailed plan for recycling that you think would work in your school or community. How would you promote your idea? Who are some people you could contact first? What resources would you need? What obstacles might you encounter?

▶ Cynthia's idea to paint the recycling bins to resemble soda cans was a clever way to entice the students at her school to recycle. Generate a list of fun and creative strategies for motivating people in your school and community to recycle. Make a poster that describes ways people can make recycling a part of their lives.

FIND OUT MORE, GET INVOLVED

Center for Clean Air Policy
444 North Capitol Street, Suite 526
Washington, DC 20001

Publishes reports on clean air issues. Write for copies.

Friends of the Earth
218 D Street, SE
Washington, DC 20003

Offers newsletters and information on ways to help the environment and a list of volunteer programs.

Kids Against Pollution
Tenakill School
275 High Street
Closter, NJ 07624

Sends out information on this networking group that works to stop pollution.

Kate Shunney

NEW LEADERSHIP
MAKES A DIFFERENCE

In addition to taking part in the leadership activities described in this chapter, 21-year-old KATE SHUNNEY *spent a semester studying at the University College Galway in Ireland. Upon her return, she wrote an article about her experience that has since been published. During her final semester at Mary Baldwin College, a women's college in Staunton, Virginia, Kate worked as the assistant editor of* Miscellany, *the school's literary magazine, and produced the largest issue of the magazine in the last twenty years of its publication. Upon graduation in 1991, Kate was awarded a Bachelor of Arts in political science with distinction and honors.*

Following graduation, Kate moved back to her hometown of Berkeley Springs, West Virginia, to live with her parents and their three dogs and to write full-time. In March 1992, she moved to Tidewater, Virginia, to work for a greenhouse company.

Kate hopes to earn a Master of Fine Arts degree and enter the teaching profession. Meanwhile, she writes poetry and pursues its publication in magazines around the country. In her free time, she writes, continues an interest in photography, and, along with her brother, remains politically active.

---

*D*URING MY SOPHOMORE YEAR AT MARY Baldwin College (MBC), I became interested in Amnesty International, an organization whose mission coincided with my growing concerns about international human rights. At the time, Amnesty International was relatively new to our campus, so the group was small. I joined, eager to become involved in a cause so in need of support. We spent much of the meeting time planning awareness activities, but the campus seemed immobile with apathy. While our events made students aware of the organization, little could be done to move the students to action on behalf of human rights. I found out later that apathy was a widespread problem on campuses all across the country.

After a hard-working but frustrating year, plans were made for the next fall. Since the leader was graduating, the group had to decide on a new chairperson. With much doubt and great anticipation, I offered to lead the chapter the next year. The members agreed and voted to make me the new chairperson.

The graduating chairperson spent a great deal of time with me. She reviewed Amnesty International's basic mission, explained the requirements of student leaders, and shared her experiences as group leader. She also told me something that both of us had seen frequently; our campus was filled with people who had the ability and desire to work on behalf of a cause, but there was a serious lack of motivation. People did not want to expend time to volunteer. The trouble was that we had a problem (human rights violations), we had vast resources (the time and talent of students), but we couldn't get the students involved enough to solve the problem.

Over the summer, I spent much of my time reading Amnesty International's constitution, making plans for group meetings, and keeping my eye on the state of international human rights. That summer, a friend from Ireland wrote to tell me that the civil war along the Republic's northern border was worsening. As a result, incidences of police brutality, legal corruption, and prison inadequacy had increased. While my friend was in no danger, much of her family lived farther north, and she feared for their safety. Having this personal connection to the importance of human rights activism gave me an even more focused approach to leading MBC's chapter of Amnesty International.

The next fall I began my junior year by arriving on campus early to attend a leadership/orientation program for campus leaders. I listened carefully to the experiences and strategies of the other chairpersons, hoping to find a way to cut through the campus apathy. In preparation for introducing a new class of students to my group, I talked with Amnesty International USA's national office. They arranged to send me information that clearly stated Amnesty International's mission and outlined how members can make a difference. With this information and some selected biographical pieces of survivors of the Holocaust, refugees from Indochina, and Soviet dissidents, I prepared myself to attract some new members. The year before, our group had eight to twelve members. In my junior year after our orientation, I had the names and numbers of 75 students who were interested in the group.

Over the next year, with the help of cooperative faculty, student members, and various community activists, MBC's chapter of Amnesty International mailed nearly 300 letters to heads of state around the world. Our letters called for the release of individuals imprisoned because of race, religion, political orientation, or affiliation. We wrote to governments in Latin America, Europe, Asia, and Africa and demanded that they uphold the United Nation's Declaration of Human Rights. By the next spring, we had been informed of nearly a dozen prisoners who had been released by the governments to which we had written.

Kate Shunney, right, with members of the Amnesty International group at Mary Baldwin College

Excited by what I saw happening, I attended Amnesty International's Mid-Atlantic Regional Conference in Washington, D.C. I hoped to meet other student leaders who had seen the same apathy and success that I had. Hundreds of college students attended, from schools near my own. We shared strategies for raising awareness and tactics in making letter-writing campaigns successful.

The conference included workshops in which activists, released prisoners, and legal professionals addressed human rights work around the world. I attended a workshop entitled "Women and Human Rights," which I thought would be of great interest to our group and the entire campus. After the workshop, I spoke with an African woman who had been imprisoned because her husband had been in a liberal political party. In prison, she had been tortured and had assumed she would be killed. Days after her imprisonment, letters from Amnesty International and other human rights organizations streamed into her prison calling for her release. Finally, the guards let her go. She reported that our work had been successful in her case, but there were many prisoners still behind walls.

Refreshed by the conference, our group's work continued. We initiated letter-writing campaigns, showed Amnesty International's tour video, and conducted an informational reception for the entire community. We invited several Peace Corps volunteers to a panel discussion in which they told of human rights conditions around the globe. We even planned to "disappear" a faculty member, to illustrate the frightening tactic of state kidnapping in Latin American countries, but this project was voted down as being a bit too disruptive.

When the year came to a close, our chapter still had many plans and much energy. Once again, however, the leadership had to be passed, as I was to leave for a semester abroad in the fall. While I was sad to leave the group, and unsure about the direction of the chapter, I knew that it was possible to solve the problems we would continue to encounter. During the year, we had recruited students with leadership capabilities to serve in a cause that affected everyone.

Even more important to me was the realization that the world could be changed—slowly, and with great effort—and that solutions existed to match the problems. The task, I had discovered, was to gather our resources (not just on our campus, but regionally, nationally, and internationally) and put them to work. And, in my vast exposure to stories of abuse and killing, I came to understand that no idea is too strange or impractical when the issue at hand is human life. Change, we had learned, only resulted from taking risks with ideas and methods.

When I left MBC for Ireland in the fall, I had a greater awareness of the human rights issues both inside the country's borders and out. Upon my arrival, the distance from home was bridged by this understanding and by my discovery that the University College Galway had its *own* chapter of Amnesty International! Small world.

There are opportunities to become involved as a leader and activist all around the globe. My experience with Amnesty International has given me confidence to venture into the world of advanced education, knowing that there are creative and nontraditional ways of reaching a goal—whether that goal is to work on behalf of human rights, or to work toward an advanced degree in your field of study. Once you become involved in leadership, opportunities of all sorts appear less intimidating. Because I took the risk of becoming a group leader, and because I saw the fruits of my labors in the form of positive change, I realized that, as they say, anything is possible.

Perhaps what is most important to remember as a leader is that you must listen. Not only must you listen to the needs of your group or organization, you must listen to the suggestions and comments of your fellow activists. In addition, it is very important to listen to your own intuition. Some of the most important ideas in problem-solving have been shelved because of fear of failure and lack of confidence. Some of the greatest setbacks have resulted from a lack of information. In order to meet our most pressing problems with successful solutions, we must listen to one another with care and respect. This will make us all better leaders, and better people.

WHAT YOU CAN DO

▶ Find out if there is a club or organization in your school or community that works for human rights. If a group exists, think about how you could contribute to it. What human and material resources does the group need to make it better? How can you get others to share your interest and join the group? If no group exists, think about what you could do to start your own.

▶ Human rights issues exist in every school and community. Identify those issues that are of interest to you. Design a plan for using local resources to address these issues.

▶ Kate's story addresses people's apathy. A lack of interest, concern, or motivation can happen in any group of people. As a leader, think about the strategies you could use to motivate others.

FIND OUT MORE, GET INVOLVED

Amnesty International
322 Eighth Avenue
New York, NY 10001

Sends information about Amnesty International's work on behalf of people imprisoned for their political beliefs.

Children of War
Religious Task Force
85 South Oxford Street
Brooklyn, NY 11217

Provides international peace leadership programs for young adults ages 13 to 18.

Oxfam America
115 Broadway
Boston, MA 02116

Offers information about Oxfam's programs that provide assistance to needy people in countries suffering from turmoil.

Save the Children
54 Wilton Road
Westport, CT 06880

Write to this organization for information on how Save the Children assists children, families, and communities in the United States and abroad.

The U.S. Committee for UNICEF
333 East 38th Street
New York, NY 10016

Provides information about UNICEF's programs that help underprivileged children around the globe.

A LEADERSHIP HANDBOOK

What Is Leadership?

$\mathcal{W}$HEN YOU HEAR THE WORD "LEADERSHIP," what do you think of? Whom do you think about? There are literally hundreds of definitions of leadership—we've included a few of them.

Leadership is the art of influencing others.

Leadership is the ability to achieve the most with the greatest cooperation.

Leadership results when others respond in a shared direction.

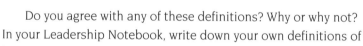

Do you agree with any of these definitions? Why or why not? In your Leadership Notebook, write down your own definitions of leadership. Title the page "My Definitions of Leadership."

• • •

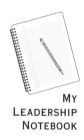

MY LEADERSHIP NOTEBOOK

A brief look at history reveals just how much our concept of leadership has changed over time. Have you ever heard of the "Divine Right of Kings"? In ancient cultures, people believed that only those born into royalty could hold leadership positions. Later, they began to believe that people were not born into positions of leadership, but were born with certain traits or characteristics of leadership. They did not believe that a person could learn to be a leader.

In the early 1900s, professionals in business and government began defining types of leadership. A leader was categorized as *autocratic, democratic,* or *laissez-faire.* Autocratic leaders, the professionals said, rule with unlimited power; they change laws when they want and make up new ones that everyone has to follow. No one challenges these leaders; people accept the fact that they have no say in making policies. "Democracy" means government by the people; democratic leaders do not make changes in policies or laws until the people approve the changes. People elect democratic leaders to represent them and their interests. Laissez-faire leaders have different polices than autocratic or democratic leaders. This third type of leader prefers to have nothing to do with policies or laws. These leaders perform only the minimum amount of work necessary.

Women and men in business management are now examining the concepts of *transactional* and *transformational* leaders. Transactional leaders use coercion or force to get others to perform. A transactional leader might say, "If you don't help the club with this project, you can no longer work with us!" Usually, people in a group do not respect this type of leader. The transformational leader, however, works hard to motivate others through enthusiasm, positive reinforcement, and genuine concern for individuals. This type of leader creates a sense of mission. Usually, transformational leaders are effective and well respected.

Today, we know that leadership ability *can* be developed and learned. It is also a fact that effective leaders can be found in people of every age, race, socioeconomic level, religion and, certainly, in both genders.

WOMEN AS LEADERS: LOOKING TOWARD THE FUTURE

*T*HROUGHOUT HISTORY, MEN HAVE dominated leadership roles, yet women are creating a new force of energy. They are actively involved as leaders in business, health care, politics, education, and sports, as well as on economic, social, and environmental issues. This involvement of all people in leadership means that you will have more opportunities to lead people and develop your leadership skills.

The outlook for women aspiring to make a difference as leaders is positive. By the year 2000:

1. More women will be elected to higher office.

2. More women will occupy top corporate posts and own successful businesses.

3. In some sports activities—particularly in long-distance events more women will achieve equality with men.

4. As women's health issues get more attention, women will become healthier.

For the last twenty years, women in the United States have taken two-thirds of the new jobs created in the information era. They will continue to do so well into the next millennium.

These predictions were made in *Megatrends 2000—Ten New Directions for the 1990's* by John Naisbitt and Patricia Aburdene (William Morrow and Company, 1992). According to the authors, both men and women have an equal chance at becoming leaders. The authors write that women have created new leadership models. These women leaders have formed a "web of inclusion" that encourages people to participate and works to exclude no one.

• • •

Use a page in your Leadership Notebook to record your own projections of women's leadership roles. What do you think women will be doing in the twenty-first century? Title your page "My Projections for Women in the Year 2000."

• • •

MY LEADERSHIP NOTEBOOK

LEADERSHIP MESSAGES ESPECIALLY FOR YOU

$\mathcal{D}$OROTHY CANTOR AND TONI BERNAY conducted in-depth interviews with 25 successful leaders. The results have been published in a book titled *Women in Power—The Secrets of Leadership* (Houghton Mifflin Company, 1992). This study revealed five wonderfully empowering messages and secrets of leadership that every leader should hear.

1. You are loved and special.

It's important to find ways that make you feel good about being you—whether that means helping someone, doing exercises, or talking to a close friend who's a good listener. Look for ways to tell yourself that you're special. Figure out which people in your life feel that same way about you. Finding people who love and respect you sets up a "feedback network." Your network of friends and family can help you feel in control of your environment. Focus on your strengths. Learn to give yourself applause. You deserve it.

• • •

In your Leadership Notebook, make a list of all the people who like you for being you.

• • •

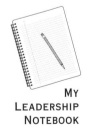

MY LEADERSHIP NOTEBOOK

2. You can do anything you want.

Work hard to overcome the message of "Girls aren't suppose to do that!" To increase your self-confidence, set small goals for yourself at first. Learn about a new topic, try a new skill, or speak to small groups. Work gradually toward a goal. Write about your feelings as you set and work toward new goals. Remember, hard work and persistence pay off!

• • •

Write about your goals in your Leadership Notebook. What steps can you take to reach those goals? Do you feel that you can accomplish anything you want? Why or why not?

• • •

**MY
LEADERSHIP
NOTEBOOK**

3. You are entitled to dream of greatness.

Sometimes, people suppress their dreams of greatness. They want to fit in with their peers or remain acceptable to friends. Look around your school, community, and state for women you want to be like. What characteristics of theirs do you admire? Share your dreams of greatness with someone.

• • •

If possible, talk with one of your role models and ask about her dreams of greatness. Write about your discussion in your notebook. You could also write a letter to that person telling her why you admire her leadership. If you want, tell her about your own dreams of greatness.

• • •

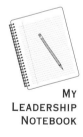

**MY
LEADERSHIP
NOTEBOOK**

4. You can use and enjoy creative aggression.

According to Dorothy Cantor and Toni Bernay, *creative aggression* means to behave in a forthright, firm manner in order to achieve an objective. Creative aggression begins with the ability to know ourselves, set limits, and assert opinions. Some young women are afraid that if they state who and what they are and what they want and need, they will threaten or destroy relationships. So they learn to be passive and agreeable in order to feel safe and fit in; they don't want to be alone. Think about what you stand for and what you're against. Don't be afraid to express your convictions!

• • •

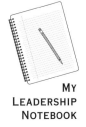

Write down your personal beliefs or convictions in your notebook. List what you value most in your life. Keep adding to your list—writing down what's important to you will help you develop a sense of self.

MY LEADERSHIP NOTEBOOK

• • •

5. You can be courageous and take risks.

Risk-taking means to take a chance on life and live to the fullest. Practice the steps toward risk-taking. Choose a risk-goal such as "speak out more at school," "start a new club," or "run for office in student government." After you've identified your risk-goal, set up a step-by-step plan to achieve it. If you don't achieve it, try to figure out what you've learned from the experience that you can use next time. And never forget that the important people in your life will always love you and consider you special—even if you fail.

• • •

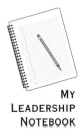

Record your risk-goals in your notebook. What are your plans for achieving these goals?

MY LEADERSHIP NOTEBOOK

• • •

LEADERSHIP OPPORTUNITIES TO CONSIDER

*Y*OU CAN FIND OPPORTUNITIES FOR leadership everywhere! Think of your school, neighborhood, community, religious affiliation, or your state. Are there changes that need to be made? How can you help to make these places better? What new ideas would you like to see implemented?

• • •

Brainstorm a list of leadership opportunities. Just let your mind think of anything and everything you'd like to change. Write down all your ideas—no matter how farfetched. Later, you can read through them and pick out the opportunities that you can take advantage of.

• • •

MY LEADERSHIP NOTEBOOK

One important characteristic of leadership is initiative, the willingness to take the first step. If you identify an area that needs to be changed or a new idea for improving your surroundings, what are you waiting for? Start on a plan of action! What people will you call on for help? What needs to be done first, second, and so on? What resources will you need? You can do it!

Changing a small piece of the world is the best way to start making a difference and leading the way for others. As you have seen from the stories in this book, you can make a difference!

WHAT TODAY'S WOMEN LEADERS SAY ABOUT LEADERSHIP

*H*AVE YOU EVER WONDERED WHAT successful women leaders think about leadership? We decided to find out for ourselves and wrote to women leaders who work in many different areas, including education, politics, journalism, sports, and science. We asked them to tell us the struggles and the rewards that leaders experience. We asked them to write down their thoughts about how they became leaders and the importance of women leaders. We also asked them to share their advice for today's girls and young women.

We compiled our list in alphabetical order and included quotations we had found in various publications. As you read these quotations, keep in mind your own thoughts about leadership. Which quotations do you agree with? Which ones sum up your own feelings about leadership? You may want to choose one of these quotations for your personal motto.

❝ Never giving criticism without praise is a strict rule for me. No matter what you are criticizing, you must find something good to say—both before and after. . . . Criticize the act, not the person. ❞

❝ Big success is nothing but a lot of little successes sitting in a row. ❞
> — Mary Kay Ash, Chairman Emeritus, Mary Kay Cosmetics, Incorporated

❝ Be the absolute best you can. ❞
> — Cathleen Black, President and CEO, Newspaper Association of America

❝ Don't try to be one of the boys. Be yourself! ❞
> — Dr. Joyce Brothers, Psychologist and Author

❝ Set your goals high and work to achieve them—and never be afraid of failure, for the tragedy comes not in failing, but in never having tried to excel. ❞
> — Rosalynn Carter, First Lady of the United States (1977-1981), Author, and Lecturer

❝ It is important that we, as women, pursue our goals and dreams—not because we are women, but because we are people with goals and dreams that shape who we are as individuals. ❞
> — Elaine L. Chao, Director, Peace Corps

❝ Love what you are doing. Believe in what you are doing. Select good people. ❞
> — Debbie Fields, CEO and President, Mrs. Fields, Incorporated

❝ Leadership is the ability to convince people that they want to do what you want them to do as if they had thought of it themselves. ❞
> — Eileen O. Ford, Co-founder, Ford Model Agency

❝ *You cannot shake hands with a clenched fist.* ❞
— Indira Gandhi, *Prime Minister of India*
(1966-1977, 1980-1984)

❝ *Keep in mind that true leadership is neither selfish nor static; it has a high and noble purpose—a commitment to accomplishment, to excellence, to high standards of personal and professional conduct.* ❞

❝ *True leadership translates itself through action and power to achieve personal success and also contributes to the public good—to the betterment of society.* ❞
— Evelyn Gandy, *Former Lieutenant Governor,*
State of Mississippi

❝ *To love what you do and feel that it matters—how could anything be more fun?* ❞
— Katharine Graham, *Chairman of the Board,*
The Washington Post

❝ *Life is a miracle, but you have to give it meaning, shape and value. Choose what you can contribute to make society better. My sister and I got our strength from our parents. We learned to keep trying until we succeeded. . . . That's perseverance.* ❞
— Marcelite J. Harris, *Brigadier General, U.S. Air Force*

❝ *Three rules for success for women:*
1. *Show up.*
2. *Hang on.*
3. *Stick around.*
In short, leaders emerge because they put themselves forward and get involved; they persevere even when times are tough; and they keep on being active. ❞
— Rosabeth Moss Kanter, *Author and Professor,*
Harvard Business School

   I am only one; but still I am one. I cannot do everything, but still I can do something; I will not refuse to do the something I can do.
     — Helen Keller, Humanitarian

   It seems to me that the single most limiting factor in a person's life is not lack of talent but lack of vision. How can we achieve what we cannot see? How we see ourselves does not have to be fixed in childhood. Whatever you think you can accomplish, think bigger; you can probably do more.
     — Judy Kinberg, Senior Producer, Dance in America

   Accept responsibility for your life and live in the present. This is encouraged by focusing on the following values: dedication to truth; delayed gratification; balance of inner and outer success.

   Follow your dreams and always remember to go for it!

   To change or not to change is a risk. You must trust and listen to yourself. Sometimes not changing is a bigger risk than change.
     — Billie Jean King, Director, World Teamtennis

   Opportunities are usually disguised by hard work, so most people don't recognize them.
     — Ann Landers, Newspaper Columnist and Author

   Women who can prove themselves capable are beginning to succeed like never before in business and politics. . . . We all have something very special to give toward our goal of a better world. We will raise our voices to give it. We will be proud, we will be strong, and we will not be denied.
     — Mary Landrieu, State Treasurer, Louisiana

❝ Our ability to find a good idea is the main illumination in our lives. A good idea is our self-esteem and our bread. A good idea is the result of our unique way of putting things together. ❞
— Frances Lear, Founder and Editor-in-Chief, Lear's magazine

❝ Leadership has nothing to do with gender. ❞

❝ Women bring to leadership situations a more consultive and nurturing approach. We have that edge over men, probably for what would appear to be obvious reason. But it wasn't too long ago that these qualities were considered weaknesses, part of the old-guard reasoning that women weren't 'tough' enough to lead anywhere or anything outside of the home. ❞
— Wilma P. Mankiller, Principal Chief, Cherokee Nation

❝ Speak up and speak out—women are shy about speaking. My motto is say it—say it again only louder and with more firmness and then say it again with a smile but don't flinch. ❞
— Barbara A. Mikulski, U.S. Senator, Maryland

❝ Decide what you do well, and work hard to sharpen those skills. These will help you make it to the top in any profession that you seek. ❞

❝ If you have the talent and skills to be the best, strive to prove that you are the best. ❞

❝ Just because a goal is not easy to attain, and you must compete to get there, does not mean that you should take the back seat to anyone. Go for it; win or lose it will be worth the effort. And sometimes in losing you learn how to win the next one. ❞
— Patsy T. Mink, U.S. Representative, Hawaii

❝ *The exhilaration of success far outdistances the disappointment of failure. Take a chance and dare to succeed.* ❞
— Josie C. Natori, President, Natori Company

❝ *Never forget compassion—the gift of responding with both wisdom and feeling. Without compassion, another's situation cannot be understood; without compassion, there is no community; without compassion, children learn only selfishness and greed; without compassion, there is no true disciple or discipline. The secret of leadership is to be fully human which is possible only by compassionate people.* ❞
— Kara Newell, Executive Secretary, American Friends Service Committee

❝ *We recognize leaders not by what or who they are . . . but by what they do.* ❞
— Ann Richards, Governor of Texas

❝ *Just as I learned through sports to put myself in the proper position for a shot or rebound, I more importantly learned to put myself in the proper position for good things to happen to me in life!* ❞
— Robin R. Roberts, National Sports Anchor, ESPN

❝ *It is not fair to ask of others what you are not willing to do yourself.* ❞

❝ *Remember, no one can make you feel inferior without your consent.* ❞

❝ *When you cease to make a contribution you begin to die.* ❞
— Eleanor Roosevelt, First Lady of the United States (1933-1945)

❝ We stand on the shoulders of those who have come before us. It is the responsibility of those of us in leadership positions to provide the shoulders for those women who will come after us. ❞
— Laura F. Rothstein, Professor of Law,
University of Houston

❝ Competition is easier to accept if you realize it is not an act of aggression or abrasion. . . . I've worked with my best friends in direct competition. Whatever you want in life, other people are going to want, too. Believe in yourself enough to accept the idea that you have equal right to do it. ❞
— Diane Sawyer, TV Journalist

❝ Dreaming is a good first step, but only you can make that dream come true by actually doing it. ❞

❝ Failure does not kill you, but wondering about what might have been because you never even tried eats away at your self-esteem and your chance for happiness. ❞
— Carole Shaw, Founder and Editor-in-Chief,
Big Beautiful Woman magazine

❝ The most important thing is to keep your confidence up. We all endure years in grammar school or high school when it seems no one—not teachers, not fellow students—feels we have any charm or promise. The following school year, a new teacher or a new friend can change all that. (For me, the change came when my fifth-grade teacher, Sophie Ravin, encouraged me to write stories.) The tough part is getting through the bad time. To a young person, a year is a long time. You have to remember that life is long, and if you want something, you have a good chance of getting it. ❞
— Amity Shlakes, Editorial Features Editor,
Wall Street Journal

❞ *Hard work, long hours and personal sacrifice are all necessary to achieve success, but the end rewards are well worth it.* ❞
 — Lillian Vernon, Founder/Chief Executive Officer,
  Lillian Vernon Corporation

❞ *Nothing happens without a dream. The most valuable thing you can do is daydream. The daydreaming mind will wander to something greater than anything your conscious mind could ever have imagined. . . . The more you visualize [your dream], the more you understand it. And in that visualization, you find a piece of it that's accessible, that you can make happen immediately. That's how you begin. Soon enough you're on the road to realizing your dream.* ❞
 — Lili Fini Zanuck, Film Director and Producer

READ MORE ABOUT IT:
A LEADERSHIP BIBLIOGRAPHY

$\mathcal{H}$AVE YOU EVER WONDERED WHAT A famous leader did before she became famous? Ever wonder how someone becomes a leader? You can discover these facts—and more—when you read a biography or autobiography. These books introduce you to people. You learn about their childhood, family, and friends. When you read biographies about leaders—or autobiographies written by leaders—you discover how and why they became leaders. Their stories tell you what inspires them and why they continue to lead others.

Look through this bibliography to find books about the women leaders you admire or have heard about. Scan through the list until you find a title that interests you or catches your imagination. To help you in your book search, we arranged this list by reading level, starting with the easiest readers.

Many of these books can be found at your local library. But if you don't find the exact one, ask a librarian. Many librarians are happy to help you find a specific title or recommend other books on the same subject. Explore on your own to find other books—and keep reading.

BOOKS FOR KINDERGARTEN THROUGH GRADE TWO

Brook, B., *Harriet Tubman* (Englewood Cliffs, New Jersey: Silver Burdett, 1990).

Selden, B., *A Story of Annie Sullivan, Helen Keller's Teacher* (New York: Dell, 1987).

Smith, K., *Harriet Tubman* (New York: Simon & Schuster, 1989).

Storr, C., *Ruth's Story* (Milwaukee, Wisconsin: Raintree Publishers, 1985).

Verheyden-Hilliard, M. E., *Engineer from the Comanche Nation* (Bethesda, Maryland: Equity Institute, 1985).

———, *Mathematician and Administrator, Shirley Mathis McBay* (Bethesda, Maryland: Equity Institute, 1985).

———, *Scientist and Administrator, Antoinette Rodez Schiesler* (Bethesda, Maryland: Equity Institute, 1985).

———, *Scientist and Astronaut, Sally Ride* (Bethesda, Maryland: Equity Institute, 1985).

———, *Scientist and Governor, Dixy Lee Ray* (Bethesda, Maryland: Equity Institute, 1985).

———, *Scientist and Puzzle-solver, Constance Tom Noguchi* (Bethesda, Maryland: Equity Institute, 1985).

———, *Scientist from Puerto Rico, Maria Cordero Hardy* (Bethesda, Maryland: Equity Institute, 1985).

———, *Scientist with Determination, Elma Gonzalez* (Bethesda, Maryland: Equity Institute, 1985).

BOOKS FOR GRADES THREE THROUGH SIX

Anderson, L., *Mary McLeod Bethune* (New York: Chelsea House Publishers, 1991).

Baker, R., *The First Woman Doctor* (New York: Scholastic, 1987).

Blair, G., *Laura Ingalls Wilder* (New York: Putnam, 1981).

Boylston, H., *Clara Barton, Founder of the American Red Cross* (New York: Random House, 1963).

Brandt, K., *Marie Curie: Brave Scientist* (Mahwah, New Jersey: Troll Associates, 1983).

Buck, R., *Tiffany Chin: A Dream on Ice* (Chicago: Childrens Press, 1986).

Bulla, C. R., *Pocahontas and the Strangers* (New York: Scholastic, 1988).

Chadwick, R., *Ann Morrow Lindbergh: Pilot and Poet* (Minneapolis: Lerner, 1987).

Davidson, M., *Helen Keller* (New York: Scholastic, 1972).

Draffron, C., *Gloria Steinem* (New York: Chelsea House Publishers, 1988).

Duden, J., *Shirley Muldowney* (New York: Macmillan Children's Book Group, 1988).

Faber, D., *Margaret Thatcher: Britain's Iron Lady* (New York: Viking Children's Books, 1985).

Fritz, J., *The Double Life of Pocahontas* (New York: Puffin Books, 1987).

Gherman, B., *Sandra Day O'Connor* (New York: Viking Children's Books, 1991).

Giff, P. R., *Laura Ingalls Wilder: Growing Up in the Little House* (New York: Viking Children's Books, 1987).
——, *Mother Teresa: Sister to the Poor* (New York: Puffin Books, 1987).

Gray, C., *Mother Teresa: Her Mission to Serve God by Caring for the Poor* (Milwaukee, Wisconsin: Gareth Stevens, 1988).

Greenfield, E., *Rosa Parks* (New York: HarperCollins Children's Books, 1973).

Hamilton, L., *Clara Barton* (New York: Chelsea House Publishers, 1988).

Haskins, J., *Diana Ross: Star Supreme* (New York: Puffin Books, 1986).
——, *Shirley Temple Black: Actress to Ambassador* (New York: Viking Children's Books, 1988).
——, *Winnie Mandela: Life of Struggle* (New York: Putnam, 1988).

Henry, S., *One Woman's Power: A Biography of Gloria Steinem* (New York: Macmillan Children's Book Group, 1987).

Hovde, J., *Jane Addams* (New York: Facts on File, 1989).

Howe, J., *Carol Burnett: The Sound of Laughter* (New York: Puffin Books, 1988).

Huber, P., *Sandra Day O'Connor* (New York: Chelsea House Publishers, 1990).

Huges, L., *Madam Prime Minister: A Biography of Margaret Thatcher* (New York: Macmillan Children's Book Group, 1989).

Hyman, T., *Self-Portrait: Trina Schart Hyman* (New York: HarperCollins Children's Books, 1989).

Ilgenfritz, E., *Anne Hutchinson* (New York: Chelsea House Publishers, 1991).

James, C., *Julia Morgan* (New York: Chelsea House Publishers, 1990).

Johnston, J., *They Led the Way: Fourteen American Women* (New York: Scholastic, 1987).

Kent, C., *Barbara McClintock* (New York: Chelsea House Publishers, 1991).

Kliment, B., *Billie Holiday* (New York: Chelsea House Publishers, 1990).

Knudson, R., *Julie Brown: Racing against the World* (New York: Viking Children's Books, 1988).
——, *Martina Navratilova: Tennis Power* (New York: Viking Children's Books, 1986).

Kudlinski, K. V., *Juliette Gordon Lowe* (New York: Viking Children's Books, 1988).

Lauber, P., *Lost Star: The Story of Amelia Earhart* (New York: Scholastic, 1988).

Lee, B., *Judy Blume's Story* (New York: Macmillan Children's Book Group, 1981).

Lefer, D., *Emma Lazarus* (New York: Chelsea House Publishers, 1988).

Levine, E., *Ready, Aim, Fire!: The Real Adventures of Annie Oakley* (New York: Scholastic, 1988).

———, *Secret Missions: Four True Life Stories* (New York: Scholastic, 1989).

Macdonald, F., *Working for Equality* (New York: Franklin Watts, 1988).

McGovern, A., *Secret Soldier: The Secret of Deborah Sampson* (New York: Scholastic, 1977).

———, *Shark Lady: True Adventures of Eugenie Clark* (New York: Macmillan Children's Book Group, 1984).

Meltzer, M., *Betty Friedan: A Voice for Women's Rights* (New York: Viking Children's Books, 1985).

———, *Dorthea Lange: Life Through the Camera* (New York: Viking Children's Books, 1985).

———, *Mary McLeod Bethune: Voice of Black Hope* (New York: Viking Children's Books, 1987).

———, *Tongue of Flame: The Story of Lydia Maria Child* (New York: Viking Children's Books, 1990).

———, *Winnie Mandela: The Soul of South Africa* (New York: Viking Children's Books, 1986).

Monroe, J., *Steffi Graf* (New York: Macmillan Children's Book Group, 1988).

Monsell, H. A., *Susan B. Anthony: Champion of Woman's Rights* (New York: Macmillan Children's Book Group, 1986).

Montgomery, M. A., *Marie Curie* (Englewood Cliffs, New Jersey: Silver Burdett, 1990).

O'Kelly, M., *From the Hills of Georgia: An Autobiography in Paintings* (Boston: Little, Brown, 1983).

Oneal, Z., *Grandma Moses: Painter of Rural America* (New York: Viking Children's Group, 1986).

Patterson, L., and C. H. Wright, *Oprah Winfrey: Talk Show Host and Actress* (Hillside, New Jersey: Enslow Publishers, 1990).

Roberts, N., *Barbara Jordan: The Great Lady from Texas* (Chicago: Childrens Press, 1984).

Rosenthal, B., *Lynette Woodard: The First Female Globetrotter* (Chicago: Childrens Press, 1986).

Sabin, F., *Amelia Earhart: Adventure in the Sky* (Mahwah, New Jersey: Troll Associates, 1983).

———, *Elizabeth Blackwell: First Woman Doctor* (Mahwah, New Jersey: Troll Associates, 1982).

———, *Young Queen Elizabeth* (Mahwah, New Jersey: Troll Associates, 1989).

Santrey, L., *Louisa May Alcott: Young Writer* (Mahwah, New Jersey: Troll Associates, 1986).

Saunders, S., *Dolly Parton: Country Going to Town* (Mahwah, New Jersey: Troll Associates, 1986).

——, *Margaret Mead: The World Was Hers* (New York: Viking Children's Books, 1987).

Shore, D., *Florence Nightingale* (Englewood Cliffs, New Jersey: Silver Burdett, 1990).

Sterling, D., *Freedom Train: The Story of Harriet Tubman* (New York: Scholastic, 1987).

Stevenson, A., *Founder of the American Red Cross* (New York: Macmillan Children's Book Group, 1986).

——, *Molly Pitcher: Young Patriot* (New York: Macmillan Children's Book Group, 1986).

Tyler, L., *Anne Frank* (Englewood Cliffs, New Jersey: Silver Burdett, 1990).

Wagoner, J. B., *Martha Washington: America's First, First Lady* (New York: Macmillan Children's Book Group, 1986).

Weil, A., *Betsy Ross: Designer of Our Flag* (New York: Macmillan Children's Book Group, 1983).

Wenzel, D., *Anne Bancroft: On Top of the World* (New York: Macmillan Children's Book Group, 1989).

White, E. E., *Jennifer Capriati* (New York: Scholastic, 1991).

Wilkie, K., *Helen Keller: From Tragedy to Triumph* (New York: Scholastic, 1983).

Williams, B., *Breakthrough: Women in Archaeology* (New York: Walker and Company, 1981).

Wolitzer, H., *Introducing Shirley Braverman* (New York: Farrar, Straus & Giroux, 1975).

BOOKS FOR GRADES SIX THROUGH NINE

Archer, J., *Breaking the Barriers: The Feminist Movement* (New York: Viking Children's Books, 1991).

Billings, C., *Grace Hopper: Navy Admiral and Computer Pioneer* (Hillside, New Jersey: Enslow Publishers, 1989).

Blau, J., *Betty Friedan* (New York: Chelsea House Publishers, 1991).

Cain, M., *Louise Nevelson* (New York: Chelsea House Publishers, 1989).

De Pauw, L., *Founding Mothers: Women of America in the Revolutionary War* (New York: Houghton Mifflin, 1975).

Haskins, K., *Katherine Dunham* (New York: Putnam, 1982).

Jones, C., *Karen Horney* (New York: Chelsea House Publishers, 1989).

Paolucci, B., *Beverly Sills: Opera Singer* (New York: Chelsea House Publishers, 1990).

Peavy, L., *Dreams into Deeds: Nine Women Who Dared* (New York: Macmillan Children's Book Group, 1985).

Rappaport, D., *Women: Their Lives in Their Words* (New York: HarperCollins Children's Books, 1990).

BOOKS FOR YOUNG ADULTS AND UP

Adam, P., *Eileen Gray: Architect Designer: A Biography* (New York: Abrams, 1989).

Allione, T., *Women of Wisdom* (New York: Viking Penguin, 1988).

Andrews, L. V., *Medicine Woman* (San Francisco: Harper & Row, 1983).

Arbur, R., *Marion Zimmer Bradley* (San Bernardino: Borgo Press, 1986).

Ash, M. K., *Mary Kay: The Success Story of America's Most Dynamic Businesswoman* (New York: HarperCollins, 1987).

Ballou, P. K., *Women: A Bibliography of Bibliographies* (Boston: G. K. Hall, 1986).

Bank, M., *Anonymous Was a Woman* (New York: St. Martin's Press, 1979).

Barkalow, C., and A. Raab, *In the Men's House: An Inside Account of Life in the Army by One of West Point's First Female Graduates* (New York: Poseidon Press, 1990).

Barrette, J. B., *Prairie Politic: Kay Orr vs. Helen Boosalis: The Historic 1986 Gubernatorial Race* (Lincoln, Nebraska: Media Publications, 1988).

Bateson, M. C., *Composing a Life* (New York: NAL-Dutton, 1990).

Beckett, W., *Contemporary Women Artists* (New York: Universe Books, 1988).

Beetles, C., *Mabel Lucie Atwell* (North Pomfret, Vermont: Trafalgar Square, 1991).

Belcher, G., and M. Belcher, *Collecting Souls, Gathering Dust: The Struggles of Two American Artists, Alice Neel and Rhoda Medary* (New York: Paragon House, 1991).

Benson, G., Jr., *Andre Norton* (San Bernardino: Borgo Press, 1990).
——, *Margaret St. Clair* (San Bernardino: Borgo Press, 1990).
——, *Marion Zimmer Bradley* (San Bernardino: Borgo Press, 1991).

Billings, C. W., *Grace Hopper: Navy Admiral and Computer Pioneer* (Hillside, New Jersey: Enslow Publishers, 1989).

Bloch, M., and G. Holcomb, *Joyce Treiman: Friends and Strangers* (Los Angeles: USC Fisher Gallery, 1988).

Bolton, S. K., *Famous Leaders among Women* (Salem, New Hampshire: Ayer Company Publishers, reprint of 1875 edition).

Boutelle, S. H., *Julia Morgan: Architect* (New York: Abbeville Press, 1988).

Burke, M. A. H., *Elisabeth Nourse, 1859-1938: A Salon Career* (Washington, D.C.: Smithsonian, 1990).

Burnett, C. B., *Five for Freedom: Lucretia Mott, Elizabeth Cady Stanton, Lucy Stone, Susan B. Anthony, Carrie Chapman Catt* (Westport, Connecticut: Greenwood Press, 1968).

Caraway, H. W., *Silent Hattie Speaks: The Personal Journal of Senator Hattie Caraway* (Westport, Connecticut: Greenwood Press, 1979).

Carey, G., *Anita Loos: A Biography* (New York: Knopf, 1988).

Carter, M., *Isabella Stewart Gardner and Fenway Court* (Boston: Gardner Museum, 1986).

Cesara, M., *No Hiding Place: Reflections of a Woman Anthropologist* (San Diego: Academic Press, 1982).

Christie, V. J., *Bessie Pease Gutmann: A Biography* (Lombard, Illinois: Wallace-Homestead, 1990).

Danilova, A., *Choura: The Memoirs of Alexandra Danilova* (New York: Knopf, 1986).

David-Neel, A., *My Journey to Lhasa* (Boston: Beacon Press, 1988).

Daviess, M. T., *Seven Times Seven* (Salem, New Hampshire: Ayer Company Publishers, 1980).

Debakis, M., and J. Bell, eds., *Rosa Alice: May Stevens: Ordinary Extraordinary* (New York: Universe Books, 1985).

Deegan, M. J., *Women in Sociology: A Bibliobiographical Sourcebook* (Westport, Connecticut: Greenwood Press, 1991).

Didion, J., *Past Imperfect* (New York: Berkley Publishing, 1985).

Dillard, A., *The Writing Life* (New York: HarperCollins, 1990).

Dryfoos, S. W., *Iphigene: My Life and The New York Times: The Memoirs of Iphigene Ochs Sulzberger* (New York: Random House, 1987).

Edwards, M. B., *Six Life Studies of Famous Women* (Salem, New Hampshire: Ayer Company Publishers, reprint of 1880 edition).

Foner, P.S., and J. F. Pacheco, *Three Who Dared: Prudence Crandall, Margaret Douglass, Myrtilla Miner—Champions of Antebellum Black Education* (Westport, Connecticut: Greenwood Press, 1984).

Forbes, M. J., and J. Bloch, *Women Who Made a Difference* (New York: Simon & Schuster, 1990).

Foster, J. O., *Life and Labors of Mrs. Maggie Newton Van Cott* (New York: Garland Publishing, 1988).

Garner, L., *A Brave and Beautiful Spirit: Dora Marsden* (Brookfield, Vermont: Gower Publishing, 1990).

Ginzburg, E. S., *Within the Whirlwind* (New York: Harcourt Brace Jovanovich, 1982).

Hall, R. K., A Place of Her Own: The Story of Elizabeth Garrett (Santa Fe, New Mexico: Sunstone Press, 1983).

Hamilton, M., Mary Macarthur (Westport, Connecticut: Hyperion Press, 1976).

Hanuse, E. J., One Step at a Time: My Walk across America (New York: Avon Books, 1988).

Harding, S., Laura Dreschler (Pittsburgh: Dorrance, 1987).

Harris, T., Jeannette Rankin: Suffragist, First Woman Elected to Congress, and Pacifist (Salem, New Hampshire: Ayer Company Publishers, 1989).

Henderson, K. U., Joan Didion (New York: Ungar, 1984).

Hetherington, S. J., Katherine Atholl 1874-1960: Against the Tide (Tarrytown, New York: Pergamon, 1989).

Hixon, D. L., Thea Musgrave: A Bibliography (Westport, Connecticut: Greenwood Press, 1984).

Hobson, L. Z., Laura Z—A Life: Years of Fulfillment (New York: Donald I. Fine, 1986).

Hurst, F., Anatomy of Me (Salem, New Hampshire: Ayer Company Publishers, 1980).

Hutchinson, L. S., Anna J. Cooper: A Voice from the South (Washington, D.C.: Smithsonian, 1981).

James, C., Julia Morgan (New York: Chelsea House Publishers, 1990).

Jenkins, B., I Once Knew a Woman: A Patchwork of Seven Unforgettable Women (Brentwood, Tennessee: Wolgemuth & Hyatt, 1990).

Jones, B., For the Ancestors; Autobiographical Memories (Champaign: University of Illinois Press, 1983).

Kaye, M. M., Sun in the Morning: My Early Years in India and England (New York: St. Martin's Press, 1990).

Keller, E. F., A Feeling for the Organism: The Life and Work of Barbara McClintock (New York: W. H. Freeman, 1983).

King, B. J., We Have Come a Long Way (New York: McGraw-Hill, 1989).

King, C., Barbara McClintock (New York: Chelsea House Publishers, 1991).

Koblitz, A. H., A Convergence of Lives (Cambridge: Birkhäuser, 1983).

Lewis, S., and M. F. Kremer, The Angel of Beale Street (Memphis: St. Luke's Press, 1986).

Lovell, M. S., Straight on Till Morning: A Biography of Beryl Markham (New York: St. Martin's Press, 1988).

Lynn, L., and G. Vesey, Loretta Lynn, Vol. I: Coal Miner's Daughter (Chicago: Contemporary Books, 1990).

Mack, J. E., and R. S. Rogers, The Alchemy of Survival: One Woman's Journey (Reading, Massachusetts: Addison-Wesley, 1989).

Mandrell, B., Barbara Mandrell: My Story (New York: Bantam Books, 1985).

Mathews, W., *Dauntless Women: Stories of Pioneer Wives* (Salem, New Hampshire: Ayer Company Publishers, reprint of 1947 edition).

Navratilova, M., and G. Vecsey, *Martina* (New York: Fawcett Books, 1986).

O'Hern, E., *Profiles of Pioneer Women Scientists* (Washington, D.C.: Acropolis Books, 1986).

Patterson, E. C., *Mary Somerville and the Cultivation of Science* (Norwell, Massachusetts: Kluwer Academic Press, 1986).

Peterson, D., *Dress Gray: A Woman at West Point* (Austin, Texas: Eakin Press, 1990).

Piquet, J., *For the Love of Tomorrow: The Story of Irene Laure* (Richmond, Virginia: Grosvenor USA, 1986).

Reep, D. C., *Margaret Deland* (New York: G. K. Hall, 1985).

Reynolds, L., *Kate O'Brien: A Literary Portrait* (New York: Barnes & Noble Imports, 1986).

Reynolds, M. D., *Nine American Women of the Nineteenth Century: Leaders of the Twentieth* (Jefferson, North Carolina: McFarland & Company, 1988).

Riddles, L., and T. Jones, *Race across Alaska: First Women to Win the Iditarod Tells Her Story* (Harrisburg, Pennsylvania: Stackpole Books, 1988).

Rinehart, M. R., *My Story* (Salem, New Hampshire: Ayer Company Publishers, 1980).

Roberts, A. V., *Louisa Elliott* (Chicago: Contemporary Books, 1989).

Sangathana, S. S., et al., *We Were Making History: Women in the Telgana People's Struggle* (Atlantic Highlands, New Jersey: Humanities Press, 1989).

Schaeffer, E., *With Love, Edith: The L'Abri Family Letters 1948-1960* (San Francisco: Harper & Row, 1988).

Schulman, S., *The Sophie Horowitz Story* (Tallahassee, Florida: Naiad Press, 1984).

Seligman, C. D., *Texas Women: Legends in Their Own Time* (Dallas: Hendrick-Long, 1989).

Shelley, M. W., *Vindication of the Rights of Women* (New York: Viking Penguin, 1982).

Shepherd, L., *A Dreamer's Log Cabin: A Woman's Walden* (New York: Dembner Books, 1981).

Shriver, P., et al., *Passing Shots* (New York: McGraw-Hill, 1988).

Smith, W. M., and E. A. Bogart, *The Wars of Peggy Hull: The Life and Times of the First Accredited Woman Correspondent* (El Paso: Texas Western, 1991).

Smyth, E., *The Memoirs of Ethel Smyth* (New York: Viking Penguin, 1907).

Stevens, D., *Jailed for Freedom* (Salem, New Hampshire: Ayer Company Publishers, 1990).

Sweeney, P. E., *Biographies of American Women: An Annotated Bibliography* (Santa Barbara, California: ABC-CLIO, 1990).

Thorp, M., *Female Persuasion: Six Strong-Minded Women* (Hamden, Connecticut: Shoe String Press, 1971).

Tingling, M., *Women into the Unknown: A Sourcebook of Explorers and Travelers* (Westport, Connecticut: Greenwood Press, 1989).

Tullis, J., *Clouds from Both Sides: An Autobiography* (San Francisco: Sierra Club Books, 1987).

Uglow, J. S., ed., *Continuum Dictionary of Women's Biography* (New York: Continuum, 1989).

Valens, E. G., *The Other Side of the Mountain* (New York: HarperCollins, 1989).

Wadsworth, G., *Julia Morgan: Architect of Dreams* (Minneapolis: Lerner, 1990).

Ward, M., *Maude Gonne: Ireland's Joan of Arc* (London: Pandora Press UK, 1990).

West, J., *The Woman Said Yes: Encounters with Life and Death* (New York: Harcourt Brace Jovanovich, 1976).

Wheeler, L. A., *Jane Addams* (Englewood Cliffs, New Jersey: Silver Burdett, 1990).

Williams, V., *Women Photographers: The Other Observers; 1990 to the Present* (New York: Random House, 1989).

Yalon, M., ed., *Women Writers of the West Coast: Speaking of Their Lives and Careers* (San Bernardino: Borgo Press, 1988).

Index

About the Authors

*F*RANCES KARNES RECEIVED HER PH.D. IN Education from the University of Illinois. She is currently Professor of Special Education at the University of Southern Mississippi, and has been part of the university faculty for two decades. She is Director of The Center for Gifted Studies and the center's Director of the Leadership Studies Program for grades 6-11.

Frances is a past president of The Association for the Gifted, a national organization. She has co-authored eight books and over one hundred journal articles on a variety of subjects including leadership, gifted children, and legal issues. Frances resides in Hattiesburg, Mississippi, with her husband, Dr. M. Ray Karnes.

*S*UZANNE BEAN RECEIVED HER B.S. IN Elementary Education from Delta State University in Mississippi and earned her M.Ed. and Ph.D. in Special Education (with an emphasis in Gifted Education) from the University of Southern Mississippi. She is currently an assistant professor of education at the Mississippi University for Women in Columbus. She is also Director of the Mississippi Governor's School, a residential program for high school students who show high intellectual, creative, and leadership potential. She was recently elected Vice Chair of the National Conference on Governor's Schools.

Suzanne has served as President of the Mississippi Association of Talented and Gifted and has participated in numerous conference and workshop presentations. She is also a consultant in the area of education of the gifted. Suzanne and her husband, Dr. Mark H. Bean, have one child, a daughter, Cameron Meriweather Bean.